OLD NYAVIYUYI
IN PERFORMANCE

OLD NYAVIYUYI IN PERFORMANCE

Seven tales from Northern Malaŵi
as told by a master performer
of the oral narrative

Collected, translated and presented with
performance directions by
TITO BANDA

Musical notation by
Mjura Mkandaŵire and Andrea Matthews

Published by
Mzuni Press
P/Bag 201 Luwinga
Mzuzu 2

ISBN 978-99960-60-32-8
eISBN 978-99960-60-33-5

The Mzuni Press is represented outside Africa by:
African Books Collective Oxford (order@africanbookscollective.com)

www.mzunipress.blogspot.com
www.africanbookscollective.com

To Messrs Chinweizu, Onwuchekwa Jemmie and
Ihechukwu Madubuike, who, in their
Toward the Decolonization of African Literature, Vol. I,
threw out the challenge that inspired this project.

And to the memory of
Enala Mvula (Nyaviyuyi, now no longer old),
who enabled me to meet the challenge.
She died too soon.

CONTENTS

EPIGRAPHS

Since these narratives [African stories] are oral ones, to ignore [their delivery and dramatic performance] is to miss one of their most significant features. The vividness, subtlety and drama with which stories are often delivered have often been noted in general terms by those who know a lot about the literature they present (as distinct form collectors who merely reproduce texts written for them by employees)...

Ruth Finnegan,
Oral Literature in Africa

One listens to a clever story-teller, as was our old friend Mungalo, from whom we derived many of these tales. Speak of eloquence! Here was no lip mumbling, but every muscle of face and body spoke, a swift gesture often supplying the place of a whole sentence...

E.W. Smith and A.M. Dale,
The Ila-Speaking Peoples of Northern Rhodesia

... [A]s editors of oral texts, we have undertaken a by no means easy responsibility of reconciling two media of cultural expression, and ... we owe at least to the culture from which we have taken something the duty not to violate our charge but to accord it as much of its integrity as the host culture will allow. For the oral culture does have some integrity...

Isidore Okpewho,
"Towards a Faithful Record on Transcribing and Translating Oral Narrative Performance."

ACKNOWLEDGEMENTS

Firstly, I am greatly indebted to Associate Professor Mupa Shumba, my colleague in the Department of Languages and Literature at Mzuzu University. It was in his vast private library at Phwezi Secondary School, where we both once taught English, that I chanced upon books which brought into focus my long-standing interest in oral literature.

My second debt of gratitude is owed to Mr Mjura Mkandawire, Malaŵi's eminent composer, who first prepared the musical notation for the songs in these tales. Between 1982 and his retirement in 1994 Mr Mkandawire taught music at Blantyre Teachers College and Phwezi Secondary School.

I am equally indebted to Andrea Matthews, from Marlboro, Vermont, USA, who arrived at Mzuzu University early July 2006 with music notation software, just in time to further refine and transcribe Mr Mkandawire's hand-written scores on computer, thereby creating the present professional quality presentation of the songs. She holds a Masters of Music Education with Kodály Emphasis from Holy Names University, Oakland, CA (USA). She spent a year of post graduate study at the Franz Liszt Academy of Music in Budapest, Hungary. She has spent the past 25 years teaching music in the Keene, New Hampshire, USA public school system.

In this remarkably opportune collaboration, Mr Mkandawire and Ms Matthews have accomplished what is the despair of many ethnomusicologists, who speak of the difficulty in notating and scoring traditional African music.

Ms Matthews is to be further acknowledged for writing the preface to and preparing interpretive notes on the songs.

Lastly, but certainly not least, I am most grateful to the Research and Publications Committee of Mzuzu University for funding the printing of this book.

INTRODUCTION

I Discover Old Nyaviyuyi

I met old Nyaviyuyi quite by chance. I had been reading *Toward the Decolonization of African Literature* in which I had come across the following challenge thrown out by the authors of that seminal work:

> Since even the best available written texts of oral literature – and they are clearly in the minority – are nevertheless limited in their success at capturing the performance dimension, scholars have a challenge before them to invent techniques, notations, formulas and codes for reproducing in writing such performance aspects of oral narrative as they have so far not been able to capture in print. The same challenge extends to both critics and writers: ...Our scholars, critics and writers have a responsibility to make innovations for reproducing oral narratives in full in writing. [1]

It was a challenge I could not ignore – both as a writer and because I knew exactly what the authors meant: I have enjoyed some splendid performances of *vidokoni* (folktales, sing. *chidokoni*); but folktales in written form – whether in Chitumbuka, Chichewa or English – have always fallen far short of giving me the joy and appreciation that I have always derived from a good oral performance. I had all but accepted the universal cry of despair by folklorists over the deficiencies of the transcribed tale vis-à-vis the oral original when I stumbled upon the above challenge and determined to take it up.

I decided I would locate a gifted oral artist as my informant. And right away it seemed I didn't have too far to look: Nyabetera, a woman of Zumara Village on the outskirts of Phwezi Secondary School in Rumphi district, where I was then an English teacher, appeared to be the obvious choice. She was the local bard; she was almost invariably the song leader at wedding celebrations, funeral vigils and various other social occasions. I had watched her perform at several such occasions and had admired her verve and artistry. It seemed most likely she was equally gifted at narrating folktales.

When I approached her with the request for a tale-telling session in her village, she was predictably enthusiastic. She in fact told me a tale right on the spot. I did not find that spontaneous narration particularly striking; nevertheless I considered it a good sign. We agreed on a date when I would go to her village and listen to more tales from her and other women.

And so one weekend in May 1988 I arrived in Zumara Village on an audition visit. Nyabetera quickly gathered her fellow women, whipping up a good deal of excitement among them as she summoned them to an occasion that was clearly no longer habitual in their village. But it rather intrigued me that even after a fairly large group of women and children had gathered before me on the packed-earth veranda of one of the houses, Nyabetera didn't think we were ready to begin until she had fetched a slight, elderly lady sporting a knitted skull cap and wearing a shy, nearly toothless smile. And although Nyabetera opened the tale-telling with a tale of her own – told with characteristic enthusiasm – it was all too apparent that she had no pretensions to being the star raconteur among the assembled women.

My first impressions of the self-effacing old lady in the skull cap gave me no reason to suspect any gift of verbal art in her. But when, after uttering not a word since she had joined the group, she laughed appreciatively at the end of the fourth narrator's tale and announced formulaically *"Chakwane!"* (Now mine), I thought I might be in for a surprise. Sure enough, the *chidokoni* she proceeded to perform (for hers was indeed a performance, not merely a narration) confirmed that I had found my informant: Here was a woman who had a huge love for *vidokoni,* and who told them with fervour and flavour. I there and then made a date with her for the following weekend.

Armed with a tape recorder, I collected two tales from Nyaviyuyi during my next visit. A lean harvest, to be sure; but that was only because several people who had turned up for that session – which was held in Nyaviyuyi's house – had to be granted the joy of listening to play-

2

backs of their own narrations or songs. That old Nyaviyuyi could, time permitting, have performed many more tales during that afternoon's four-hour session is indicated by this remark from her after we had agreed on yet another date: *Sono kwiza ndiko mwizengeko luŵiro, kuti nyengo yakwimbira yiŵenge yikuru"* (But do come in good time, so that we have enough time for tale-telling).

The way old Nyaviyuyi responded to play-backs of her performances during that initial recording session seemed to me a clear indication of the artist in her. In sharp contrast with the others in that gathering, whose response generally was little more than giggly fascination at hearing their own voice, she invariably responded to her play-backs with a calm, engrossed excitement: She would rock to the beat of a tale's song as though she were leading the singing all over again, her lips silently forming the words as she listened along. At the beginning of a play-back of hers she would snap into a rapt posture which she would maintain throughout until I would click the stop button at the end of the tale.

 One other point that right away impressed me about old Nyaviyuyi that afternoon was her sensitivity to the quality of her audience's choral response during the songs accompanying her tales. Faulty response (i.e. failure to respond according to her prior instructions) quite often led to a breakdown in her narration, a breakdown from which she recovered only after considerable coaxing to continue with the tale. This intense artistic discrimination in her solidified my conviction that I had chanced upon a real virtuoso of oral narrative performance.

A further point that testified to old Nyaviyuyi's genius for the oral narrative performance was her intuitive grasp of the importance of mime in the genre. This was revealed in a remark she made during the performance of a tale after I had been working with her for nearly a year. The tale was about how, by a fiendish trick, Kalulu the Hare scared all the animals and humans away from the neighbourhood's well: He dug a hole in a strategic spot near the well. In this hole he buried the whole of himself – except his front teeth, which were left jutting out of the

3

ground. The macabre sight of teeth protruding from the earth, plus a song issuing from underneath the teeth that spoke of the earth having sprouted teeth, was enough to keep man and beast well away from that water. Although she had lost all her front teeth, old Nyaviyuyi felt compelled to enact by mime the way Kalulu's teeth jutted out of the earth: *"Sonimurongoraninge nchende!"* (I'll have to expose my tooth-lessness), she said apologetically and proceeded to perform the mime: She threw back her head and bared her toothless upper front gums, placing two upward-pointing fingers against them – much to the amusement of her audience.*

I was also struck, right from the outset, by the way old Nyaviyuyi achieved vivid and arresting description in her performances through exceptionally well employed onomatopoeia and idiophones.** In fact, it was principally her adept use of the idiophone that made me know for certain that I had stumbled upon a true enthusiast for the oral narrative performance; for, as Fortune has rightly observed. "To be used skillfully, [idiophones] must correspond to one's inner feeling. Their use indicates a high degree of sensitive impressionability."

As if to endorse what I had already concluded about old Nyaviyuyi's enthusiasm for narrative performance, one of her daughters-in-law said towards the end of that first recording session: *"Yewo dada, mwatisanguruskira ŵabuya"* (Thank you sir for cheering up our granny).

"You feel she has been cheered up?" I asked her.

---

*The reason why this tale is not included in this collection throws further light on old Nyaviyuyi as a performer of the oral narrative. I failed to tape the initial performance of this tale: Although the tape was running throughout the performance, it turned out that, due to some malfunction, the machine had not been recording. I later taped three retellings, each time hoping to get as fine a performance as the initial one. But all the three narrations were singularly flabby – thin in narrative texture and lacking Nyaviyuyi's trade-mark stylistic devices. This was consistently the case whenever I asked her to retell a tale, whether to the same audience or not, on the same day or not. Quite clearly, freshness was a prerequisite for this particular performer's literary artistry.

**The sounds of Nyaviyuyi's idiophones contribute so much to the impact of her performance. That is why, for the benefit of readers not familiar with the phonetics of a Bantu language, I felt I should provide at the top of each translated tale a simple, lay-man's guide to the sounds of all the idiophones used in the tale (arranged in order of their occurrence). Before reading any tale, therefore, such readers will find it helpful to first take a look at its idiophone guide.

"Very much so," she replied assuredly. "You need only look at her eyes: When ŵaNyaviyuyi's eyes glint like that, it shows she is in high spirits."

A little earlier I had overheard this same lady (who was in a group sitting outside by the door, listening in as old Nyaviyuyi performed within) observe: *"Nthena ŵaNyaviyuyi ŵakondwa chomeni"* (That's Nyaviyuyi at her happiest).

This matter of mood reveals yet another dimension of Nyaviyuyi's inborn skills in oral narrative performance. As I indicate in the head notes for the tales in this volume, Nyaviyuyi performed each tale in a particular mood. It was quite apparent that these moods were dictated by the tales themselves and had nothing to do with Nyaviyuyi's humour on the various days that the tales were recorded, for her general disposition was invariably cheerful. Quite clearly then, the various moods were deliberately chosen by this gifted oral artist to suit each tale.

Taking up the Challenge

I have said above that this project was inspired by the challenge thrown out to scholars and writers by Chinweizu et al to "invent techniques, notations, formulas and codes for reproducing in writing such performance aspects of oral narratives as they have so far not been able to capture in print." I must admit though that it was with much trepidation that I set out to take up the challenge. Pronouncements of despair by experts in the field gave me the feeling I was presuming to rush in where angels feared to tread. To quote but one such pronouncement:

> ...It is clear how *impossible* (my emphasis) it is to convey in a written version the vivid and varied representations of scene or atmosphere which can be evoked by the spoken narration and enactment, particularly where the story-teller is skilled in his art. This illustrates once again the point that any bare synopsis of plot or any written translation, whether literal or paraphrased, can never catch the flavour of the actual occasion when the

story was performed with and to a group, nor fully represent what, for a Limba, is assumed to play such a large part – the actual dramatic process of story-telling.[3]

Was it true, I wondered, that the written word was all that incapable of·describing the tale performer's tone and speed of voice, his or her mime, facial expressions, gestures and other performance aspects? Admittedly, much would have to be lost through the process of transcription/translation. But why should it be impossible to communicate through the printed word the drama one witnesses during a narrative performance? Surely it shouldn't be so difficult to set down what one saw, heard and felt during a tale-telling session, much less so if the narrator was a skilled performer. Certainly it should be relatively easy to accomplish this if, along with the text, and *within* it. the transcriber/translator reported on the salient auditory and visual components of the tale's performance.

Story-telling is indeed a dramatic process as other scholars besides Finnegan also point out. Soko makes the following observation about the Tumbuka folktale narrator: "The Tumbuka narrator assumes the role of an actor, especially as far as body movements and the art of manipulating the voice are concerned."[4] To underscore his point, Soko quotes from an article by Calame-Griaule titled "Ce qui donne du gout aux contes" (that which gives taste to tales), in which the latter bemoans the complete disappearance from translated [and transcribed] tales of "... the play aspect, the dramatization of the tale; gestures, attitudes, facial expressions of the narrator... In a nutshell, what gives taste to the tale, just as salt and spices give taste to food...."[5] It would therefore seem only natural that, just as the dramatist, through stage directions, reports on the action of his play, transcribers/translators of oral narrative performances would also – through what one might call performance directions – report on the oral delivery of the tale. Transcriptions/translations of oral narratives would then have to look and read much like play scripts; for, as Kral points out in his *Plays for Reading*, "In good plays, the script replicates real discourse."[6]

This is by no means to suggest that transcribing/translating oral narrative performance in this way will convey all "the vivid and varied representations of scene or atmosphere which can be evoked by the spoken narration and enactment."[7] But surely it would convey more of these elements and thereby bring the written version much closer to the actual performance than providing just the tale text, even if the text were accompanied by performance annotations tacked away in commentaries, footnotes or headnotes.

Let me cite but three instances where, by providing performance directions within the text in the manner of a play script, transcribers/translators would have brought us so much closer to the oral performance. To begin with, Finnegan has the following headnote for one of the stories included in her *Limba Stories and Story-Telling:*

> The extreme personality of the girl in the story, whether in joy or sorrow, was conveyed by the mode of delivery as well as by her words and actions, and the whole narrative was made dramatic by the narrator's presentation and acting. [8]

Surely, Finnegan could have *shown* us the girl's extreme personality by describing, in performance directions within the text, the mode of delivery employed by the performer at every joyful or sorrowful experience the girl encounters in the tale? And, although the girl's words are duly quoted and her actions narrated, we would have been brought even closer to the original oral performance if Finnegan had at every point described, again in performance directions within the text, the narrator's dramatic presentation and acting.

Elsewhere in the same volume Finnegan is a little more helpful to her readers. The following performance direction, although relegated to a footnote, does bring the reader fairly close to the original oral performance: "This was related very quietly, conveying the atmosphere of night, sleep, and stealth." [9]

The reader's sense of loss is even more acute when a transcriber/translator fails to bring him close to the highly emotional atmosphere in which a praise poem is performed. Such a failure is demonstrated by Mapanje and White in their anthology *Oral Poetry from Africa.* In an end-of-book note intended to give the reader "the context of the original performance"[10] the editors say of one section of "Shaka", a praise poem on the illustrious Zulu king: "The five-fold repetition in the lines which follow is overwhelmingly impressive in performance."[11] (The lines referred to read: "He who while devouring some devoured others/And as he devoured others he devoured some more."[12] Now, rather than this generalized statement, surely what is needed is for the reader to be shown, through descriptive performance directions within the text, exactly in what respects the repetition of the lines is "overwhelmingly impressive in performance."

In their introduction to the anthology, Mapanje and White pose the following questions:

> Can oral poetry be written down? What happens when the performer can no longer look his audience of friends and fellow-townsmen straight in the eye? What happens when his gestures, his shifts in tone and emphasis, his use of topical allusions, his whole game with his audience, have all to be supplied in private by an anonymous reader helped by an editor's notes?[13]

In my view the problems implied by these questions get mitigated to a significant extent if the anonymous reader is helped by internal performance directions. Editorial notes alone, even when the reader is advised to use them "with imagination, bearing in mind above all that what appears on the page is but an echo of something that happened in performance....,"[14] won't do much to bridge the gap between the written text and the original oral performance.

Apparently this supposed impossibility of capturing in print the performance aspects of an oral narrative is so intimidating that it can confuse the perspective of even well-intentioned scholars. Take, for example, the case of a keen academic enthusiast for oral literature, Steve Chimombo, Professor Emeritus of English, University of Malawi. In his *Malawian Oral Literature: The Aesthetics of Indigenous Arts*, Chimombo includes an analysis of an oral narrative performance, claiming that such an analysis is "a closer approximation of the original performance than the published collections."[15] He presents a transcription of the Chichewa version of "The Hare and the

Well" and a parallel English translation before going into a detailed analysis of the performance, which he personally attended.

While it may be true that Chimombo's analysis is closer to the original oral performance than versions of the tale so far published, I contend that the professor could have got even closer to the original performance of the tale than he does in his analysis. He does not get as close as he could have simply because he is one of those who believe in the impossibility of capturing in print the performance aspects of an oral narrative. Speaking of the story-teller's performance of the tale, Chimombo informs us:

> There were elements of drama here: acting, gesticulation, change of facial expression and tone of voice. These important elements are not seen in the transcript as there is no method of presentation which could be made apart from filming the performance.[16]

Chimombo then goes on to discuss tone of voice, especially the variation that occurred in it to include irony, humour, sarcasm, seriousness and mockery. He claims that it would be idle to go into where exactly tone of voice suggested any of these moods, "as this would require apparatus for measuring and recording."[17] Maybe. But then he goes on to describe the narrator's change of voice in quality and pitch in the dialogues: Elephant's voice was "dignified and deliberate", Hyena's was "hoarse and whining", and Hare's was "high, small and delivered faster than any other animal's speech."[18] Surely, if these descriptions of voice changes were given at points where they occur within the text the reader would get more of the tale's flavour than from a text that does not include them.

Even more helpful to the reader would have been the information contained in the following paragraph were it provided within the text. (Ironically, the paragraph opens with the words "It is in the gestures that the narrator excelled himself", making the discerning reader wonder why the gestures, if they were so impressive, were not described within the text):

> ...He did not actually stand up and act, but was shifting and moving in considerable agitation as he got carried away with the role he was play-

ing. This was especially so when he acted Fisi (Hyena) being frightened by Kalulu (Hare) at the well. *Iih, walisesa liwilo* ("did he run fast), ... and, coming slowly back to check that the zombie was gone: *nde ndinabwera, kuchita ngati kuwenda, kubisala chonchi, kuyang'ana, kuyang'ana* ("so I came back stealthily, hiding like this, and I looked this way and that").[19]

"Hiding like this": Without internal description of how the narrator mimed the manner of hiding, these words hardly achieve any communication. "I looked this way and that": Internal description of the narrator's movements that accompanied these words would get the reader much closer to the original oral performance. The reader ought to be *shown* within the text exactly how "the narrator introjected (sic) himself into the story and identified himself with the various characters."[20]

There are those who would argue that performance directions within the text would disrupt reading continuity and therefore negatively affect the reader's enjoyment of the tale. That would certainly be the case were we dealing with a genre like the short story, for example. But we are talking about oral literature, a genre which, like the play, is meant to be appreciated as *performance*. Much will therefore be lost in the printed version of such a genre if auditory and visual elements are not given precedence over other considerations.

Finnegan is emphatic about the role of the story-teller in this regard. She points out that it is the story-teller who gives his tale effectiveness "by his delivery and enactment of the plot."[21]

We really cannot hope to capture in print much of the impact or effectiveness of the original oral narrative if we exclude from it the central aspects of delivery and enactment. In my view, exclusion – for whatever reason – of the delivery and enactment aspects from a transcribed or translated tale is a serious form of disruption of the readability of the tale, precisely because it robs it of its impact and effectiveness.

Isidore Okpewho, another prominent name in African oral literature scholarship, urges editors of oral literary texts to represent them with "due propriety."

> ... This propriety implies that, since part of the business of the oral literary scholar seems to be to establish the peculiar poetics of this genre of literature (understandably as against that of written literature), a considerable amount of care should be given to highlighting some of the things that add up to its uniqueness. Perhaps it should be stressed that, as editors of oral texts, we have undertaken a by no means easy responsibility of reconciling two media of cultural expression, and that we owe at least to the culture from which we have taken something the duty not to violate our charge but to accord it as much of its integrity as the host culture will allow.... [22]

The integrity of oral literature lies in the auditory and visual elements of its performance. Ignoring to highlight these elements when transcribing or translating oral texts merely because we are anxious to preserve the integrity of the written medium of cultural expression would certainly be a violation of our charge.

Similarly, with regard to the songs that accompany folktales it has always puzzled me that tale collectors almost invariably seem to be content with publishing only the lyrics of the songs, and not their music. Here again there are cries of dismay within scholarship:

> Just as with translation, nothing can replace the actual singing of the songs in the many *cante fables* in this collection. In some future ideal world, a tape or disc of the songs will be fitted into an envelope attached to the back cover of publications such as this.... [23]

Why, though, can't the reader, while awaiting that ideal world, be given the music notations and scores of the tales' songs? Readers can then sing the songs themselves, or, if they cannot read music, learn the songs from having them sung by someone who can read music. Neglecting to include notes with the lyrics not only denies the reader the joy of learning these usually very tuneful songs, but also considerably reduces the aesthetic and emotional impact of the tales themselves.

As for my work with old Nyaviyuyi, hindsight leaves me in no doubt that even if I had begun working with her without the challenge of Chinweizu and others in mind, the wish to transmit to the reader the sheer verve and drama of her performance would have imposed the play-script technique on my transcription and translation of her tales. I am convinced that in the face of the superb artistry of this competent raconteur, in the face of her splendid skill in leading the singing of the songs that accompany her tales, it would have been inevitable for me to experience the humility Birago Diop felt before his *griot*, Amadou Koumba. He tells us:

> If I have not succeeded in transmitting to the tales the same atmosphere in which I, as the listener, and those whom I watched were plunged, atten- tive, shuddering, or rapt in reverie ... it is because I lack the voice, the verve and the powers of mimicry of my old griot.[24]

And so, short of presenting a sound film or video of old Nyaviyuyi in performance, I feel mounting the transcriptions and translations of her tales in the style of a play script and providing music notation for the songs in the tales is the closest I can get to making available to the reader "the voice, the verve and the powers of mimicry" of this splen- did artist of the oral narrative.

In concluding this section of the introduction, let me once again quote that doyen of Africa's oral literature, Ruth Finnegan; for what she says in the following observation about Limba stories also applies to the tales in this volume, and therefore further justifies the manner in which I have presented them:

> From one point of view, perhaps, Limba stories about people or animals are only simple ones; to some, indeed, the written translations here may seem to represent only a rather crude form of art; the stories are relative- ly short, uncomplicated, and lacking in certain of the characteristics of a sustained piece of written literature.... But when one also takes into account the artistry of the actual narration of these tales ..., then ... their complexity begins to emerge. To grasp their literary impact one must go beyond the actual text to the whole dramatic process of the story-telling, which gives them so much of their meaning and subtlety.[25]

A Word on the Songs

In translating the song texts, an attempt has been made to come up with a rendering that makes it possible, generally, to sing the English texts to their respective tunes.

Italics in the English lyrics indicate words and expressions whose meanings were not readily apparent to the translator, as well as to the narrator herself. (However, in tale number 7, *Chidyamtambo* would literally mean 'eater-of-the-sky'. It seems, therefore, that the word refers to the giant bird – the owner of the eggs. *Walilima* would then mean 'is approaching with sound and fury'. But since this is only speculation, I have left the two words untranslated).

In most cases these untranslatable words are entirely foreign to the Chitumbuka language. John Pepper Clark-Bekederemo makes the following observation on the use of foreign words in African oral literature:

> Their power of evocation lies in the fact that they are exotic... The same can be said for [the use of foreign words in songs]. The theme song of Ofe the Short, Chief of the conspirators against the house of Ozidi, is a famous example. It conveys no precise meaning, yet its effect is electric upon an Ijo crowd.[26]

Thus in order that all may appreciate the musical effect of these untranslated words, the following simple guide to the phonemes of vowels and certain consonant clusters has been provided for the benefit of readers not familiar with the phonetics of a Bantu language:

a	as in above
e	as in let
i	as in see
o	as in Rome
u	as in rule
gh	as r in the French *ronde*
ph	as first p in principle
th	as th in Thames (River)

A Portrait of the Artist

Old Nyaviyuyi's life story is nearly as enthralling as the tales she spins in this volume. But while her tales depend for their impact on her superb ability to sketch a picture with word and gesture, her life story enthralls more because of its content than the artistry with which she narrated it.

Childhood

Enala Mvula ('Nyaviyuyi' is only a nickname – inherited from her paternal grandmother – that has stuck remarkably well) was born at Khondowe (Livingstonia) Mission Station of the then Free Church of Scotland in Rumphi district, Northern Malawi. She could not tell the year of her birth; but she recalled that her father, Peter Mvula, was at the time working at the station, herding the mission cattle. *"Wakaliskanga ng'ombe za Sing'anga"* (He was herding the Doctor's cattle) is how she put it – a reference to Dr. Robert Laws, the Scottish missionary who was the founding head of Livingstonia Mission. From this remark, and in view of her aged looks when I began working with her, one would place her birth somewhere between 1910 and 1915.*

Enala spent her early years partly in her father's village at Ng'onga in Rumphi's Henga Valley, and partly at Tchesamu in Mzimba district. And she had vivid memories of some terrible experiences at the latter place, where she had stayed with her maternal grandmother.

It seems the way she was treated by her grandmother left much to be desired. She was being fed so inadequately that, to stay the pangs of hunger, she would resort to eating maize husks and other food residues she foraged at the village dumping ground. Sometimes she would even eat clods of soil she dug up from a salt lick.

She recalled with particular poignancy one incident when she almost

---

*Old Nyaviyuyi died in 1999, six years after I had left Phwezi. Her son, Titus Zunda Mzumara, told me that towards the end of her life she had been afflicted with dementia.

died: She and the other little girls of the village had gone into the bush to pluck the leaves of the *chilowe* shrub for relish. As the girls picked the leaves, Enala, famished as usual, saw an exposed root of the shrub. Thinking the tuber was edible, she proceeded to eat it.

In a graphic account, Nyaviyuyi told me how she passed out after she had eaten some of the root. She was carried back to the village and laid in her grandmother's house, where the next morning found her still unconscious, people having filled the house in the meantime, as they had begun to give up hope that she would ever live. Breaking into impeccable Chingoni, the language of Tchesamu in those days, Nyaviyuyi narrated how the relieved villagers greeted her eventual return to consciousness: "'*Umtwana wayabheka!*' (the child has opened her eyes) they said."

Enala's father eventually had her returned to Ng'onga. But as she had by now reached school-going age, she was soon sent to Luzi, just across the South Rukuru River from Ng'onga, there to stay with an uncle so that she could attend Chololo School. Unfortunately, her schooling was to be cut short after only three years due to a problem that bedeviled that area in those difficult days – banditry. The pupils were in daily peril of being attacked by gangs of rogues that terrorized the area. And Nyaviyuyi described how she and a group of other pupils were one day set upon by brigands who seriously injured one of the pupils. This attack forced the closure of the school for security reasons.

"Wakaŵa Luzi yula, dada!" (Luzi was a terrible area in those days, sir) she commented bleakly. *"Chiuta watimbamo luswazu mu Luzi"* (God has lashed Luzi with a whip of pacification).

Then the marriage of Enala's parents broke up. Her mother, Mary Nyamnyasulu, returned to her home area of Usowoya in the hills to the east of Henga Valley, taking her only two children (Enala and her elder sister) with her. There she remarried.

Adolescence and Marriage

Enala's adolescence was all too brief. It was long enough, however, for her to learn from her mother to love *vidokoni*. For Mary Nyamnyasulu was a popular *vidokoni* performer. According to Nyakamshati, Nyaviyuyi's half-sister, she used to be asked to perform "wherever she went." She was even nicknamed "Nyakachindundu", after a *chidokoni* she liked to tell about the chindundu ant. And in her turn Enala taught her fellow children to love *vidokoni*. Speaking of Nyaviyuyi, Nyakamshati told me: *"Ka mbeneŵaŵa ndiwo Ŵakati- sambizga vidokoni. Ŵakatenge 'Zani pano timbe vidokoni'; mbwenu tafika"* (it's none other than she herself who taught us *vidokoni*. She would say 'Come, let's sing *vidokoni'*; and we would come).[27]

Enala's adolescence was abridged because she was a precocious child. Even while she was still playing mother, her ideas and her knowledge of various domestic chores were those normally expected of a mature woman. She told me that her first husband, Timoti Mzumara, wooed her while she had a doll strapped to her back, and that she was so young that the suitor had to use older girls as intermediaries in speaking to her! As a matter of fact, Mzumara betrothed her before she came of age; so that immediately he learnt she had had her first period he went and eloped with her.

One further intriguing thing about this child-bride is that the marriage she contracted was a polygamous one – she was a second wife. But even more intriguing is the fact that when her husband died Nyaviyuyi was inherited by the eldest son of her co-wife, a fact she mentioned without embarrassment: *"Ndine wakwamba kuchita ntheura?"* (Am I the first one to have had this type of marriage?) she asked.

Yet another interesting episode in Nyaviyuyi's life story is as follows: When she first got married, her people received from the Zumaras only one cow as her *lobola* (bride price), while custom stipulated five head of cattle. To compound the situation, the beast died before very long. Then Nyaviyuyi's people cut up the carcass and delivered the meat to the Zumaras, a gesture intended to get the latter to understand

16

that the cow's untimely death meant the Zumaras had yet to pay the *lobola*. But the bride price was still unpaid when Nyaviyuyi's husband died and she married the son of her co-wife.

Nyaviyuyi's *lobola* was still being awaited when at one time she went on a visit to her people. She was in the late stages of pregnancy during that visit, and in fact delivered while still with her people.

When her mother-in-law went up from Henga Valley to see the baby, Nyaviyuyi's uncle (for she had grown up in her mother's home area) asked why the older lady had come up into the hills. Upon being told she had come to see the new-born Zumara baby, the man declared that the Zumaras had no baby there (implying that they had no claim to Nyaviyuyi's baby as they still hadn't paid the bride price). Whereupon Nyaviyuyi weighed in with the announcement that she would always regard herself as being married to the Zumaras, even if her *lobola* was still being awaited from them. She let it be known she would never be married anywhere else. When her uncle heard this, he threw a tantrum and, swearing a terribly binding oath, said she could go wherever she pleased, but should never set foot in his village again. Nyaviyuyi told me she then and there set about preparing her baby's *nthembe**, getting ready to go back to the Zumaras the following day.

But the following morning, before Nyaviyuyi could depart for Henga Valley, the issue was brought before the elders of the village and her uncle was found to be in the wrong. He acknowledged being at fault, and there and then he and Nyaviyuyi drank of the *mphamba*** potion to undo the terrible oath he had pronounced against his niece. Then Nyaviyuyi returned to her marriage, which remained *lobola*-less to the day she passed away.

---

*   Container in which a mother keeps plain water – *daŵali* – (for very young babies) or light maize porridge (for older ones). Traditionally this is a gourd container, and various medicinal roots against gripe and other infant ailments are immersed in the water or porridge. Additionally, the roots give the drink a most appetizing flavour.

**   To undo an oath of prohibition, all the parties involved are required to partake of this potion. Unless this ritual is observed, ignoring such an oath will result in the parties dying of terrible boils covering the whole body.

"Ya-Nyaviyuyi"

Nyaviyuyi's second husband died in 1975. She had five children with him, while she had only one with her first husband. Four of her children are still alive, one of them – a son, her last-born with her second husband – together with his two wives, looked after her till her death.

Old Nyaviyuyi explained to me that one reason she had kept her marriage despite all odds was that she had had great admiration for her father-in-law. Of him she enthused: "He remained an honourable man to his grave."

The gap left by her father-in-law's passing seemed to have been well filled by solicitous daughters-in-law, not to mention affectionate grandchildren who in her old age used to chummily refer to her as "ya-Nyaviyuyi" – jolly old Nyaviyuyi.

TITO BANDA
Department of Languages and Literature
Mzuzu University

September 2006

REFERENCES

1. Chinweizu, Onwuchekwa Jemie and Ihechukwu Madubuike, *Toward the Decolonization of African Literature Vol. I* (Enugu: Fourth Dimension Publishers, 1980), p.83.
2. G. Fortune, *Idiophones in Shona* (London: Oxford University Press, 1962), p. 6.
3. Ruth Finnegan, *Limba Stories and Story-Telling* (London: Oxford University Press, 1967), p. 85.
4. Boston Soko, "Translating Oral Literature into European Languages: The Folktale", in Richard Whitaker and Edgard Sienaert (eds.), *Oral Tradition and Literacy* (Durban: Natal University Oral Documentation and Research Centre, 1986), p. 115.
5. Ibid, p. 118.
6. Thomas Kral, *Plays for Reading* (Washington, D.C.: United States Information Agency, 1994), p. iv.
7. Finnegan, op cit p. 85.
8. Ibid p. 117.
9. Ibid p. 135.
10. Jack Mapanje and Landeg White (eds.), *Oral Poetry from Africa* (Harlow: Longman, 1983), p. 174.
11. Ibid, p.182.
12. Ibid, p. 26.
13. Ibid, p. 3.
14. Ibid, p. 6.
15. Steve Chimombo, *Malawian Oral Literature: The Aesthetics of Indigenous Arts* (Zomba: Centre for Social Research, University of Malawi, 1988), p.83.
16. Ibid, p. 115.
17. Ibid, p. 115.
18. Ibid, pp. 115-116.
19. Ibid, p. 116.
20. Ibid, p. 117.

21. Finnegan, op. cit. p. vii.
22. Isidore Okpewho, "Towards a Faithful Record: On Transcribing and Translating the Oral Narrative Performance": Paper presented at the Sixth Ibadan African Literature Conference, 27 July – 1 August, 1981.
23. Daniel J. Crowley, in the Foreword to Mable H. Ross and Barbara K. Walker, *"On Another Day..." Tales told among the Nkundo of Zaire* (Hamden, Connecticut: Archon Books, 1979), p. 13.
24. Birago Diop, *Tales of Amadou Koumba* (Harlow: Longman, 1985), pp. xx-xxi.
25. Finnegan, op. cit. p. vii.
26. John Pepper Clark-Bekederemo, *The Ozidi Saga* (Ibadan University Press and Oxford University Press Nigeria, 1977), p. xxix.
27. Personal communication with Nyakamshati, 15 October, 1988.

THE TALES IN ENGLISH

1. A Hunter's Magic

This tale was performed in the sitting room of my house at Phwezi Secondary School around mid-afternoon. Nyaviyuyi's audience consisted of the author and six girls, all children of teachers at Phwezi. She sat on a palm carpet, the tape recorder placed on a stool before her. Her audience sat about her around the tape recorder.

Guide to Idiophone Sounds

kutu-kutu: ku as coo in cool; tu as too in tool
kha!: as kha in khaki
tembe-tembe: te as ta in tale; mbe as mbe in embezzle
yii!: as yea in yeast
ongh!: approx. an oh ending in a guttural grunt
thi!: th as th in Thames (river); i as ee in bee.

(Nyaviyuyi was light-hearted throughout this performance)

MS NGOZA was married to a man who had the magical habit of turning into a lion. She, of course, had no idea he was that type of man.

After they had settled down as husband and wife the man one day sets off for the forest. "Relish," he tells his wife by way of explanation. "I'm going to look for relish."

On arrival in the forest the man shakes his whole body with a giant spasm *kutu-kutu-kutu,*

(At the idiophone kutu-kutu-kutu NARRATOR vigorously shakes her entire trunk)

an action which at once causes him to turn into a lion. The beast then begins to sing as follows:

(NARRATOR leads the singing in stately, self-assured tones while rocking away to the rhythm of the melody):

NARRATOR: Ah-ha-ha let an eland come now
AUDIENCE: *Ndombole ya matete, ndombole*
N: Ah-ha-ha it's all for my Ngoza
A: *Ndombole ya matete, ndombole*
N: Ah-ha-ha meat's her only relish
A: *Ndombole ya matete, ndombole*
N: Ah-ha-ha bwenkha* she's said No to
A: *Ndombole ya matete, ndombole*
N: Ah-ha-ha, aaah, *haya we!*
A: *Ndombole ya matete, ndombole*
N: Ah-ha-ha, aaah, *haya we!*
A: *Ndombole ya matete, ndombole*
(NARRATOR speaks in applauding tones:)
There comes an eland, sure enough, materializing from nowhere! The lion instantly kills it *kha!* It then feasts voraciously on the carcass, leaving only a hind leg. Thereafter the beast shakes

---

*   A type of vegetable sauce of the consistency of okra. Here bwenkha is used metaphorically to stand for all vegetable sauces, which Ngoza won't touch, preferring meat instead.

itself *kutu-kutu*, turning at once into a man again. Then he carries the heavy leg *tembe-tembe*,

(At the idiophone tembe-tembe NARRATOR mimes the action of carrying a heavy load on the shoulder)

and returns to the village.

(In delighted tones:)

"Hurray, here comes relish!" his wife cries out when she sees him as he enters the village. She runs to him and receives the meat.

(In a droning voice:)

"The wild animals had almost finished up their kill," the man says to his wife. "All I found was this leg. But I said to myself,'No matter: I'm lucky to have at least found something.'" (Whereas it's he himself who has feasted on the eland!)

The meat is duly consumed.

The next day –

(In a droning voice:)

"Er, I'm off again. I'd better go and look for relish." Thus he goes to the forest. There – *kutu-kutu*, he turns into a lion. He goes

(Singing:)

N: Ah-ha-ha let a zebra come now
A: *Ndombole ya matete, ndombole*
N: Ah-ha-ha it's all for my Ngoza
A: *Ndombole ya matete, ndombole*
N: Ah-ha-ha meat's her only relish
A: *Ndombole ya matete, ndombole*
N: Ah-ha-ha bwenkha she's said No to
A: *Ndombole ya matete, ndombole*
N: Ah-ha-ha aah, *haya we!*
A: *Ndombole ya matete, ndombole*

Well, the beast kills the zebra that does appear. It devours it, leaving only a hind leg. Then *kutu-kutu*, it turns into a man, who carries the meat home.

But now Ms. Ngoza begins to wonder.

(NARRATOR speaks in a sing-song voice that is charged with suspicion:)

"Aah, this husband of mine always brings home a hind leg," she says to herself. "What does it all mean? Well, we shall see."

The next day –

(In a droning voice:)

"My dear, I'm off again. Relish is quite a problem these days." Off our man goes to the bush.

This time Ms Ngoza follows her man at a distance, taking care not to be seen by him. She says,

(In a tone of determination:)

"Today I want to see how my husband hunts."

Arriving in the forest, the man as usual shakes himself *kutu-kutu* and turns into a lion. Ngoza witnesses the transformation. Our man-turned-lion goes –

(Singing:)

N: Ah-ha-ha let an eland come now
A: *Ndombole ya matete, ndombole*
N: Ah-ha-ha it's all for my Ngoza
A: *Ndombole ya matete, ndombole*
N: Ah-ha-ha meat's her only relish
A: *Ndombole ya matete, ndombole*
N: Ah-ha-ha bwenkha she's said No to
A: *Ndombole ya matete, ndombole*
N: Ah-ha-ha aah , *haya we!*
A: *Ndombole ya matete, ndombole*
N: Ah-ha-ha aah , *haya we!*
A: *Ndombole ya matete, ndombole*

(On completion of the song NARRATOR presses her forefingers under her eyes and pulls the skin down, thereby causing the eyes to open wide. At the same time she grotesquely droops the corners of her mouth. This mime signifies absence in a mocking manner – in this case absence of response from the summoned animal)

Yii! – total silence.

Our shocked lion/man tries again:

    (Singing:)

N: Ah-ha-ha let a zebra come now

A: *Ndombole ya matete, ndombole*

N: Ah- ha-ha it's all for my Ngoza

A: *Ndombole ya matete, ndombole*

N: Ah-ha-ha meat's her only relish

A: *Ndombole ya matete, ndombole*

N: Ah- ha-ha bwenkha she's said No to

A: *Ndombole ya matete, ndombole*

N: Ah-ha-ha aah, *haya we!*

A: *Ndombole ya matete, ndombole*

N: Ah-ha-ha aah, *haya we!*

A: *Ndombole ya matete, ndombole*

    (In a mocking tone:)

Ongh! – absolutely no sign of prey. There's nothing to it but for our lion/man to turn back into a human being.

    Ngoza says,

    (NARRATOR speaks in a rapid, tremulous, fear-filled voice:)

"Oh my God! So that's what my husband does!" She then runs all the way to the village.

    On reaching the village, Ngoza promptly finds a mortar and pours some maize into it. Then she invites her fellow women, saying,

    (NARRATOR speaks in enthusiastic tones:)

"Come let's pound katiki-tiki*, so I can teach you a nice pounding song I've just learnt." The women then commence pounding – *thi!thi!thi!*

    (At each thi! NARRATOR mimes a pestle going in and out of a mortar)

And Ngoza goes

(NARRATOR leads the singing with skittish zest:)

N: Ah-ha-ha let an eland come now

A: *Ndombole ya matete, ndombole*

N: Ah-ha-ha let a zebra come now

A: *Ndombole ya matete, ndombole*

N: Ah-ha-ha it's all for my Ngoza

A: *Ndombole ya matete, ndombole*

N: Ah-ha-ha meat's her only relish

A: *Ndombole ya matete, ndombole*

N: Ah-ha-ha bwenkha she's said No to

A: *Ndombole ya matete, ndombole*

N: Ah-ha-ha aah, *haya we!*

A: *Ndombole ya matete, ndombole*

N: Ah-ha-ha aah, *haya we!*

A: *Ndombole ya matete, ndombole*

    Ngoza's husband picks up the excited katiki-tiki sounds from afar as he approaches the village.

    On reaching the edge of the village he is utterly shocked to find that the women are pounding to the tune and words of his hunting song. He can even hear his wife's companions exclaim

    (NARRATOR speaks in excited tones:)

"Eh-eh! You've brought a most interesting pounding song, Ms Ngoza!" All of which completely drains the strength out of him.

    Ngoza's husband sits down in a hidden place and listens to the women's singing, thinking as he listens:

    (In a forlorn voice:)

"So my wife spied on me today. No wonder game did not respond to my call. That is the end; I shall no longer be able to kill animals."

Come night the people of the village turn in, each couple to their own house.

And in Ngoza's house her husband says to her:

---

*   A manner of pounding whereby two or more women pound maize in one mortar at the same time, rhythmically striking the grain with their pestles one after another.

(With sarcasm:)
"My dear wife, that pounding song you were singing this afternoon is very nice. It particularly suits those of us who are hunters. How about singing it for me now?"

Ms Ngoza says within herself,
(In an alarmed voice:)
"Oh dear! So my husband heard us singing!"

Try as she may to diffuse the situation by acting sweetly and by lying that she has forgotten the song, her husband insists on her singing it. And so Ngoza goes –
(NARRATOR leads the singing in a thin, fear-strangled voice:)
N : Ah-ha-ha let an eland come now
A: *Ndombole ya matete, ndombole*
N: Ah-ha-ha let a zebra come now
A: *Ndombole ya matete, ndombole*

N: Ah-ha-ha it's all for my Ngoza
A: *Ndombole ya matete, ndombole*
N: Ah-ha-ha meat's her only relish
A: *Ndombole ya matete, ndombole*
N: Ah-ha-ha bwenkha she's said No to
A: *Ndombole ya matete, ndombole*
N: Ah-ha-ha aah, haya we!
A: *Ndombole ya matete, ndombole*
N: Ah-ha-ha aah, haya we!
A: *Ndombole ya matete, ndombole*

No sooner does Ngoza finish off singing than the man shakes with a giant spasm *kutu-kutu* and turns into a lion. Within minutes he devours his wife flesh and bone.

(With a mocking snigger:)
Thus bringing her sauciness to a sorry end! End of tale.

2. Maliro and the River Spirit

This tale was performed in the sitting room of my house at Phwezi Secondary School around mid-afternoon. Nyaviyuyi's audience consisted of the author and six girls, all children of teachers at Phwezi. She sat on a palm carpet, the tape recorder placed on a stool before her. Her audience sat about her around the tape recorder.

Guide to Idiophone Sounds

kha-kha: kha as kha in khaki

(This tale was performed in a haunted, dismal, almost spell-binding tone of voice)

A GROUP of village boys went for a swim in a river pool. In the course of their splashing and dipping, one of them – Maliro by name – laughs.

It so happens that the boy's toothy laugh attracts the attention of Chipili, the river spirit.

(NARRATOR holds her chin and leers as she speaks in lascivious tones:)

"Well, well, what lovely teeth that boy has!" says Chipili as he secretly looks on.

Irresistibly drawn by the beauty of the boy's teeth, the river spirit begins to stalk him.

(NARRATOR speaks rapidly:)

All at once it pounces on the boy and drags him down to its home in the depths of the pool.

The rest of the boys return to the village. And on arrival they report to the grown-ups:

(NARRATOR speaks in tones of childhood innocence:)

"We've come back without Maliro.
He simply vanished as we were swimming."

The villagers then launch a thorough search for Maliro. But the boy is nowhere to be found. Eventually they give him up for dead and hold a funeral for him.

Then one day, after the people have long stopped mourning Maliro, a boy named Mdangu sets out from the village and goes down to the river to cut some reeds.

Arriving at the edge of the fateful pool, Mdangu sets to work, his cutlass going *kha-kha, kha-kha*

(At the idiophone kha-kha NARRATOR swings an imaginary cutlass to and fro before her)

as he cuts his reeds.

All of a sudden he hears singing from the depths of the pool. It goes:

(NARRATOR leads the singing in a piteous, piping, child-like voice:)

NARRATOR: O Mdangu you've come back

AUDIENCE: You've come, you've come *msesese*

N: Go tell dear mother mine

A: You've come, you've come *msesese*

N: That she'll find Maliro
A: You've come, you've come *msesese*
N: Held in this deep dark pool
A: You've come, you've come *msesese*
N: On account of his fine white teeth
A: You've come, you've come
msesese
To which Mdangu replies, saying:

(NARRATOR's singing tone changes from a sad one to one reflecting enthusiastic eagerness to help:)

N: Yes, without fail
A: *Dede*
N: I will go and tell it
A: *Dede*
N: To your dear mother
A: *Dede*
N: That she'll find Maliro
A: *Dede*
N: Held in this deep dark pool
A: *Dede*
N: On account of his fine teeth
A: *Dede*

Then Mdangu returns to the village. There he reports to the grown-ups:

(NARRATOR speaks in bewildered, child-like tones:)

"I've had a strange experience at the river today. As I was cutting reeds next to the pool, someone began to sing right inside the pool. He was singing about Maliro being held under the pool on account of his teeth."

The elders do not believe the boy; they tell him that he must have been dreaming.

Mdangu, of course, knows he has not been dreaming. However, the elders' refusal to believe what he has told them makes him decide to return to the river — to confirm to himself that there is indeed someone that sings in the pool.

And so he returns to the river. He begins *kha-kha, kha-kha,*

(NARRATOR swings the imagi-

nary cutlass to and fro) cutting reeds. Then, sure enough, singing rises again out of the pool:

(Singing)

N: O Mdangu you've come back
A: You've come, you've come *msesese*
N: Go tell dear mother mine
A: You've come, you've come *msesese*
N: That she'll find Maliro
A: You've come, you've come *msesese*
N: Held in this deep dark pool
A: You've come you've come *msesese*
N: On account of his fine white teeth
A: You've come, you've come *msesese*
Mdangu responds:

(Singing:)

N: Yes, without fail
A: *Dede*
N: I will go and tell it
A: *Dede*
N: To your dear mother
A: *Dede*
N: That she'll find Maliro
A: *Dede*
N: Held in this deep dark pool
A: *Dede*
N: On account of his fine teeth
A: *Dede*

When Mdangu again reports to the elders about the mysterious singing at the pool, they are less unbelieving than before.

(NARRATOR speaks in sombre tones:)

"Let's go down to the river and check for ourselves this thing the child is talking about," they say one to another.

And so a few elders, among them Maliro's parents, and Mdangu himself go to the river. There Mdangu tells them to stand by and listen while he cuts some reeds.

As Mdangu goes *kha-kha, kha-kha,*
(NARRATOR swings the imaginary cutlass)

cutting reeds, the song of the pool comes
up again:

(Singing:)

N: O Mdangu you've come back
A: You've come, you've come *msesese*
N: Go tell dear mother mine
A: You've come, you've come *msesese*
N: That she'll find Maliro
A: You've come, you've come *msesese*
N: Held in this deep dark pool
A: You've come, you've come *msesese*
N: On account of his fine white teeth.
A: You've come, you've come *msesese*

(NARRATOR speaks in tones of shocked relief:)

Yes, indeed! The elders have heard
for themselves: Their child has been
captured by Chipili!

They return to the village.

*(NARRATOR speaks in tones
that reflect great exertion:)*

They spare no effort in gathering the
many sacrificial objects, including a
white calico cloth.

Returning to the river, they cast the
white cloth and the other items into the
pool. Whereupon a current brings
Maliro up from the depths of the pool
and deposits him onto the bank. End of
tale.

3. The Monkey/Woman

This tale was performed in the sitting room of my house at Phwezi Secondary School at mid-afternoon. Nyaviyuyi's audience was made up of the author, one woman (Nyaviyuyi's half sister) and nine children, three of them Nyaviyuyi had brought along from her village and the rest children of teachers at Phwezi. Nyaviyuyi sat in an arm-chair (as did her sister), the tape recorder placed on the coffee table before her. The children sat on the floor.

Guide to Idiophone Sounds

ndolololo: ndo as ndo in indolent; *lo* as in low

kwe!: as qua in quake, but sharper

to!: as to in told

junyunthu!: ju as ju in jute; *nyu* as in new;
    nthu approx. as ntle in mantle

hihi: hi as hee in heed

ayo! a as ah; *yo* as yo in yoke

sala! as sala in salamander but with the vowels
    more drawn out

e! as e in let

(The mood for this performance was dreamy and the pace rather lethargic)

A YOUNG man took a wife by way of elopement. He did not know that the woman had the habit of turning into a monkey that stole from people's gardens. She would stealthily repair to the bush, and there she would turn into a monkey, complete with a long tail that hung *ndolololo.*

(At the idiophone ndolololo a CHILD giggles in the audience)

Then she would forage about in people's fields. After foraging her fill, she would give her long tail a sharp tug – *kwe!* The tail would then get cut, which event would at once transform her back into a human being. Whereupon she would return to the village.

The result of this habit of hers was that she was always so stuffed with stolen pickings that she never ate sima*

Now people in the village began to wonder, saying:

(NARRATOR speaks in a sing-song, suspicion-charged voice:)

"But what does this woman eat? Aah, we shall now spy on her whenever she leaves the village."

And so one day they spy on her. She goes to the bush as usual and there transforms herself into a monkey.

---

* Malawi's staple dish (spelt *sima* in Northern Malawi, *nsima* in the rest of the country).

(In a conspiratorial tone of voice:)
The people are watching it all.

(Back to normal voice tone:)
She goes about stealing from people's fields.

Later the same day, having eaten to her satisfaction, she gives her tail a sharp tug so that she can turn into a human again. This time, however, the tail fails to get cut, and thus the transformation doesn't occur: The magic can't work any more, as she has been spied upon.

(In mocking tones:)
Pull the tail this way and that as she may, *to!* – to no avail.

(In tones reflecting emergency:)
"Dear me! What do I do now?"

(In frantic tones:)
The monkey/woman bounds to the village. There she finds an axe and then returns to the forest. She sits on a log, trailing her tail on the stump so that she might the better chop it. But first she sings:

(NARRATOR leads the singing in plaintive tones:)
NARRATOR: O my tail get cut, *tila!*
AUDIENCE: *Tendengala tila*
N: My tail get cut, *tila!*
A: *Tendengala tila*
N: O marital bliss was mine!
A: *Tendengala tila*
N: O marital joy was mine!
A: *Tendengala tila*

[Now she begins to chop at her tail with the axe. But the axe won't even make a dent in the tail; it only goes *jun-yunthu!*, as though it were a hammer. Each blow, however, hurts intensely, causing the monkey/woman to whimper (*hihi!*) and shriek out (*ayo!*) with pain].*
She moves onto another log and tries again:

(Singing:)
N: O my tail get cut, *tila!*
A: *Tendengala tila*
N: Get cut, *tila!*
A: *Tendengala tila*
N: O marital bliss was mine
A: *Tendengala tila*
N: O marital joy was mine
A: *Tendengala tila*

(NARRATOR executes two quick hand claps and then shoots her arms upward, jerking her trunk as if she is going to fly from her sitting position. All this in mime of the desperate action the protagonist is going to take next:)
Up a tree the monkey/woman swings *sala!* – thinking that up there she might manage to cut her tail: The tail just has to be cut, so she can become a human again. She says,

(In lamenting tones:)
"I had settled down to a happy married life with my husband: Mine was marital honour; mine was marital dignity...."

(Singing:)
N: O my tail get cut, *tila!*
A: *Tendengala tila*
N: My tail get cut, *tila!*
A: *Tendengala tila*
N: O marital bliss was mine!
A: *Tendengala tila*
N: O marital joy was mine!
A: *Tendengala tila*

(NARRATOR speaks in taunting tones:)
The tail just won't get cut! So that there is nothing to it but for our monkey/woman to continue foraging in people's fields.

Then one man, after the monkey/woman steals from his maize field, devises a plan: He takes a cob of green maize and hangs it in a tree. Then

---

* This paragraph is really a rendering into English of the second movement of the song (see the corresponding Chitumbuka tale number 3). The movement does not appear in the English translation because, besides the untranslatable words of the chorus, it consists of only idiophones.

he lurks nearby.

On seeing the maize cob, our monkey/woman makes a grab for it. Then the man manipulates his

arrow – e!

(Simultaneous with the idiophone e! NARRATOR flicks a finger to indicate the despatch with which the arrow was loosed upon the monkey/woman)

(In mocking tones:)

She dies on the spot. End of tale.

4. The Boy and the Monster

This tale was performed in Nyaviyuyi's house in the late afternoon. Her audience consisted of the author, two women, two young men and six children. Nyaviyuyi sat on her packed-earth floor, the tape recorder placed on a low stool before her. Her audience sat about her around the tape recorder.

Guide to Idiophone Sounds

pha-pha pha: p as first p in principle; *ha* as ha in hard.

phwililili!: p as first p in principle; *hwi* as whi in whisper; *li* as lea in lean.

kweche!: kwe as qua in quake; *che* as che in check.

kokoolololo: ko as co in cone; *lo* as in low

lililili: li as lea in lean

ng'we: ng' as ng in sing; *we* as in way.

wa!: as wa in wasp.

ngwe: ng as ng in angry; *we* as in way with a long vowel.

mbwi!: mb as mb in amble; *wi* as wi in win

wa-wa-wa-wa: as wa in wasp

go!: as in go

thenyu!: the as tha in Thames (river); *nyu* as new

siki-siki: si as in see; *ki* as *kee* in keen

phi: p as first p in principle; *hi* as hi in hinge

jenjerere: je as je in jelly; *nje* as nje in inject; *re* as ray

thi!: th as th in Thames (river); *i* as i in little

kang'aaa!: ka as ca in calm; *ng'* as ng in sing; aaa as in long ah

nchi-nchi-nchi: as nchi in munching

ng'onomo: ng' as ng in sing; the *o's* as in oh

upfu!: the *u's* as oo in fool

hee: as ha in haste

(This entire tale was performed in a sprightly, cheerful strain)

THERE CAME a very big bird. It was so unusually huge that the whole country was terrified by the sheer size of it. Everyone was certain it was a bird of ill omen. It was therefore decided that it must be killed so that the country might avert whatever calamity the huge creature portended.

And so the paramount chief summoned chiefs from all corners of his country to a meeting in his village to discuss how the monstrous bird might be killed. The royal village filled up *pha-pha-pha* with chiefs, their counsellors and the best bow-men in the land.*

They tried to kill the great bird by this method and that, but to no avail. And in his desperation the paramount chief pledged to surrender his throne to whoever managed to kill the feathered giant.

Then Funkhamakhwelu, a small

---

* The first two paragraphs of this English version are more of a paraphrase than a translation of the original Chitumbuka. This is because Nyaviyuyi opened the tale in so truncated a manner that a strictly faithful translation would adversely affect meaning.

boy of the paramount chief's village, steps up before the assembled dignitaries and says,

(NARRATOR speaks in a shrill, timid voice:)

"Let me try."

(NARRATOR waves her hand dismissively:)

"Away with you!" the incensed paramount chief tells the little one. "How dare you – a mere child – speak of trying something chiefs and master bow-men have failed to do?"

But there are some in the august gathering who think differently:

(In a resigned voice:)

"Let him try too," they say. And a heated argument arises among the chief's elders. Eventually they let the boy try.

Now, in trying, Funkhamakhwelu shoots his small arrow *phwililili!*

(At the idiophone phwililili NARRATOR thrusts an arm towards the roof)

- straight up to the great bird hovering high over the royal village. The arrow disappears *kweche!*

(At the idiophone kweche! NARRATOR gestures with an upward-thrusting finger of her still-raised hand)

into the huge bird. Then the giant bird goes *kokoolololo.*

(At the idiophone kokoolololo NARRATOR gestures with flourishing arms how the feathered creature plunges lifelessly toward the earth)

The amazed onlookers then say to the paramount chief: "See? The one you despised has killed it. What will you now do? You have to surrender your throne to the boy."

But the paramount chief says:

(In a dismissive tone:)

"Aah! What he has done is not great enough to entitle him to my throne. He would have to kill the destructive and thunderous killer Lightning to really deserve so distinguished a prize."

The infant prodigy responds to the challenge there and then. He shoots an arrow high into the clouds, the home of Lightning. The arrow finds its target and lightning goes *lililili.*

(At the idiophone lililili NARRATOR gestures with flourishing arms how Lightning plummets to a flashing but thunderless death)

But the paramount chief pronounces the killing of Lightning as not enough of a feat if the prize is to be his throne. He now says: "Jiwundembo, the man-swallowing monster – that is our real foe. It has decimated this country's population by swallowing alive whole families and sometimes whole villages.

(In a challenging tone:)

If he would succeed to my throne, let him go and find that dragon and slay it."

That is how Funkhamakhwelu sets out to find the monster Jiwundembo. He carries some salt with him and brings along his five dogs: Nkharamu [lion], Nthoromi [leopard], Makokota [leftovers of sima at the bottom of the cooking pot after the sima has been ladled out], Chimthiko [big cooking stick] and Nyerenjani [spice].

When Funkhamakhwelu arrives at Jiwundembo's den in the early evening, the monster welcomes him with a great show of hospitality. The boy is fully aware, however, that the wily ogre is planning to swallow him alive if he falls asleep during the night. Little does the monster realize though that it is Funkhamakhwelu's strategy to carefully study it during the night so as to determine how best to kill it in daylight the next day.

During the night then, thinking the boy is fast asleep, the monster decides time has come to gobble up its prey. But Funkhamakhwelu is keeping a wakeful eye on Jiwundembo's great single tooth. When the great tooth looms *ng'we!*
(At the idiophone ng'we!
NARRATOR briefly dangles a forefinger from her toothless upper gums to mime the length of the monstrous tooth)
over him, ready to strike, Funkhamakhwelu stealthily shoots out a hand toward the hearth in the centre of the cave and *wa!* – flings a fistful of salt onto the embers there.

(NARRATOR speaks in a gruff voice:)
"Hruung! What's happening to the fire?" the ogre growls, much jolted by the sudden spattering explosions among the embers.

(In a piping voice)
"I don't know," Funkhamakhwelu says, thereby indicating to the monster that he is wide awake.

Thus whenever Jiwundembo thinks Funkhamakhwelu is asleep and the monstrous tooth looms *ng'we!* over him, the boy shoots out his hand towards the hearth and *wa!* – sprays salt on the embers. The ogre's beastly designs are thereby repeatedly thwarted.

Now when day breaks *ngwe* the following morning, the monster sits down and thinks:
(In a gruff voice:)
"I've failed·to swallow this human during the night. I must think of another way of getting him." And it doesn't take the crafty ogre long to hit upon a stratagem.

The monster climbs into a tall tree and *mbwi!* – shits a heap of dung in a crotch up there. The dung quickly attracts flies, just as the ogre has schemed it. And soon the crown of the tree buzzes *wa-wa-wa* with the flies.

Then the monster returns to its den – where Funkhamakhwelu is busy planning how to attack his adversary – and says to the boy:
(In a supplicatory voice:)
"Please go and extract honey for me from a hive in that Nyamthwewo tree."

(NARRATOR points in the distance through the open door)

Funkhamakhwelu agrees. But he takes the precaution of bringing along one of his dogs – Nkharamu. He then climbs the tree.

Hardly does it dawn on him that the wily Jiwundembo has played him a stinking trick when he notices that the fiend has already arrived at the foot of the tree and is chopping the trunk with a huge axe.

(Singing in ominous tones:
At the idiophone go!
NARRATOR swings a huge imaginary axe:)

NARRATOR: It goes *go!*

AUDIENCE: You'll get killed today, you'll get killed

N: It goes *go!*

A: You'll get killed today, you'll get killed

N: It goes *go!*

A: You'll get killed today, you'll get killed

(NARRATOR speaks rapidly:)

Just as the tree cracks *thenyu!* and begins to fall, the munthyenkhu bird commands it: "Nyamthwewo, O tree, do not fall: You were not planted by Jiwundembo; you were planted by God!" The tree obeys and stands firm again – *siki-siki.*

(At the idiophone siki-siki NAR-RATOR holds up both arms rigidly and shakes her trunk to mime the firmness and upright-ness of the tree)

Funkhamakhwelu now begins to summon the dogs he left behind. He calls:

(NARRATOR leads the plain-tive singing, swaying her body to and fro to mime the gravity of the situation:)

N: O Makokota, *yalira*

A: *Hee yalira*

N: And Nyerenjani, *yalira*

A: *Hee yalira*

N: I'll get killed, *yalira*

A: *Hee yalira*

All the while the monster is hacking at the tree:

(Singing:)

N: It goes *go!*

A: You'll get killed today, you'll get killed

N: It goes *go!*

A: You'll get killed today, you'll get killed

N: It goes *go!*

A: You'll get killed today, you'll get killed

(NARRATOR speaks rapidly:)

Scarcely does the tree signal its fall by cracking *phi!* when the munthyenkhu bird says, "Nyamthwewo you were planted by God: stand firm!" And the tree indeed stands *siki-siki.*

(WOMAN in the audience inter-poses with a smile: "What lies folktales tell!")

Then the boy calls:

(Singing:)

N: O Chimthiko, *yalira*

A: *Hee yalira*

N: And Nyerenjani, *yalira*

A: *Hee yalira*

N: I'll get killed, *yalira*

A: *Hee yalira*

So far, so good. Only one dog now remains to be summoned by name.

All the while the fiend is chopping:

(Singing:)

N: It goes *go!*

A: You'll get killed today, you'll get killed

N: It goes *go!*

A: You'll get killed today, you'll get killed

N: It goes *go!*

A: You'll get killed today, you'll get killed

(NARRATOR speaks rapidly:)

No sooner is the tree heard cracking than it is commanded by munthyenkhu not to fall.

It then stands firm again.

The boy calls:

(Singing:)

N: O Nthoromi, *yalira*

A: *Hee yalira*

N: And Nyerenjani, *yalira*

A: *Hee yalira*

N: I'll get killed, *yalira*

A: *Hee yalira*

So far so good. All his dogs have now arrived. They stand *jenjerere*

(At the idiophone jenjerere NARRATOR gestures with her arms how the dogs stand in readiness to leap into action to save their master. At the same time she makes fierce puckers on her brow to mime the fierceness of the dogs)

around the tree, thereby surrounding Jiwundembo.

(In satisfied tones:)

"Aaah, now is the time," says Funkhamakhwelu.

(NARRATOR speaks rapidly:)

He shoots a fast arrow: Right into Jiwundembo's heart it goes *thi!*

(At the idiophone thi! NARRATOR jabs a finger into her own side)

And Mr Jiwundembo tumbles over *kang'aaa!*

(At the idiophone kang'aaa! NARRATOR mockingly mimes with outstretched arms the supine posture of the lifeless monster).

Cut the monster open!

(NARRATOR makes a slashing sweep with an imaginary knife)

Young men and young women, old men and old women step out of the ogre's belly. *Nchi-nchi-nchi!*

(At the idiophone nchi-nchi-nchi! NARRATOR gestures with floating movements of her hands to indicate the size of the great crowd)

To show Funkhamakhwelu their gratitude for rescuing them from the monster's belly these people carry their deliverer shoulder-high as they make their way through the forest towards the paramount chief's village. Funkhamakhwelu sings out with pride as he is borne along:

(NARRATOR leads the gay singing in swaggering tones that are punctuated with triumphant jerking of her body:)

N: "Go and slay Fierce Bird"

A: *Hee Nyamalimba tema*

N: I went forth and slew it

A: *Hee nyamalimba tema*

N: "Go and slay Lightning"

A: *Hee nyamalimba tema*

N: I went forth and slew it

A: *Hee nyamalimba tema*

N: "Go slay Jiwundembo"

A: *Hee nyamalimba tema*

N: I went forth and slew it

A: *Hee nyamalimba tema*

Those in the paramount chief's village – among them all the chiefs and master bow-men, who are still awaiting the outcome of this one-boy expedition against the monster – hear Funkhamakhwelu's song from afar.

(In a foreboding tone:)

Then the paramount chief orders that a deep grave be dug and that the soil from the digging be hidden not too far from the pit. He also orders that a mat be spread over the grave to conceal it.

When the joyous procession carrying Funkhamakhwelu arrives in the village the treacherous paramount chief speaks deceptively to the boy, telling him that he is being welcomed as a hero who, in slaying the moster Jiwundembo, has saved the entire country. He then asks Funkhamakhwelu to sit on the mat so that they may proceed to crown him paramount chief of the land.

Funkhamakhwelu has barely sat on the mat when *ng'onomo!*

(At the idiophone ng'onomo!
NARRATOR mimes the action

of suddenly falling into a pit.)
– he tumbles into the grave!

(NARRATOR speaks rapidly:)
Then they quickly bury him alive! As for the people Funkhamakhwelu has rescued from the belly of Jiwundembo, they are summarily shared out among the assembled crowd. The whole place resounds with cries of

(NARRATOR speaks in shrill, enthusiastic tones:)
"These are mine! These are mine!"

But all of a sudden Funkhamakhwelu's dogs stand *jenjerere* around the unsuspecting crowd!

(NARRATOR mimes with a fierce face and a grunt to show that devastation is about to occur. Then she breaks into screaming, serves-them-right tones:)
Wreak havoc, dogs! Wreak havoc upon the gathering! The enraged dogs slaughter the entire multitude *upfu!*

(At the idiophone upfu!
NARRATOR passes her hand across her mouth to indicate a total wipe-out)
Then the dogs turn their attention to their master's grave, and in no time they exhume him alive!

(Triumphantly:)
And so Funkhamakhwelu became ruler of that country! End of tale.

5. A Crab's Revenge

This tale was performed in Nyaviyuyi's house in the late afternoon. Her audience comprised the author, two women, two young men and six children. Nyaviyuyi sat on her packed-earth floor, the tape recorder placed on a low stool before her. Her audience sat about her around the tape recorder.

Guide to Idiophone Sounds

fya!: as fia in fiasco.
hu-uuu!: the u's as oo in hood

(The mood of the performer throughout this tale was vivacious and gay)

NKHALA THE CRAB was passing by a certain village's millet-threshing ground where a woman was busy winnowing some millet. He decided to stop awhile and watch the woman as she rhythmically worked her winnowing basket.

While Nkhala is listening to the music of the woman's winnowing basket from a hidden spot, he notices that various birds are alighting at the threshing ground. The woman is shouting *fya!* at them, shooing them away lest they begin to eat some of her millet.

Having watched the winnowing to his satisfaction, Nkhala resumes his leisurely trip towards his home in a nearby stream.

Unfortunately for Nkhala, the woman happens to see him as he is crawling across the powdery *mwelero* (millet chaff). She pauses in her winnowing, finds a stick, and with it flicks Nkhala off the threshing ground

(NARRATOR grimaces with assumed revulsion as she gestures with a flicking hand:)

"Away with you!" the woman says. "Damn you! Fancy that even the likes of you should come to bother us here!" Nkhala is sorely annoyed at being treated so rudely by the woman. He is particularly hurt by her terribly cutting 'even-the-likes-of-you' remark.

(NARRATOR speaks in bitter tones:)

"Why did she not use such a remark when shooing away those birds?" Nkhala wonders as he crawls along towards the stream. Arriving at the stream, Nkhala sits down and continues to brood upon his unpleasant encounter with that woman. Before long his bitterness extends beyond one woman to the entire village. He begins to consider how best to punish the village for the abusive treatment he has suffered there.

As it is the dry season and the village has only one water hole from which the people draw their water for domestic use, Nkhala decides he will conceal himself in the water hole and scare the people away from using it.

Thus when the village women next come to draw water from the well, they hear a fearsome roar issuing from under the water. For Nkhala is down there, going –

(Singing: At each hu-uuu, NARRATOR crouches, puffs out her cheeks to a grotesque shape and produces a deep guttural growl:)

NARRATOR: Hu-uuu! There's a village

AUDIENCE: *Yaya lero kumangalengale*

N: Hu-uuu! that abused me

A: *Yaya lero kumangalengale*

N: Hu-uuu! at their millet [threshing ground]

A: *Yaya lero kumangalengale*

N: Hu-uuu!

Terribly frightened, the women flee from the water hole and return to the village with empty water pots. There they tell the menfolk about the terror at the water hole.

(NARRATOR speaks in incredulous tones:)

"What terrifying thing can be in a well?" the men ask. "Come along and show us."

The women go back to the water hole with the men.

(In measured, ominous tones:)

Scarcely does one woman touch the water with her gourd dipper when up again comes the terrifying growl from the depths of the well.

(Singing:)

N: Hu-uuu! There's a village

A: *Yaya lero kumangalengale*

N: Hu-uuu! that abused me

A: *Yaya lero kumangalengale*

N: Hu-uuu! at their millet

A: *Yaya lero kumangalengale*

N: Hu-uuu!

(NARRATOR executes two quick hand-claps to mime frightened urgency)

In great terror they all bolt and return to the village.

(In a serves-them-right tone of voice:)

The poor village suffers unspeakably with regard to water. The people are at a loss what to do.

Then one day, while the people are still moaning about their water problem, Kalulu the Hare visits the afflicted village.

"I'll see what I can do to help you," says Kalulu after the villagers have told him about their suffering.

Then Kalulu scampers straight to the water hole. There Nkhala reveals his identity to his fellow animal.

(NARRATOR speaks with bitter relish:)

"Those people treated me most rudely at their millet-threshing ground. They will yet regret!" he tells Kalulu.

After chatting thus with Nkhala, Kalulu runs back to the distressed village.

"I know how to deal with your problem," he tells the villagers. "Come with me to the stream and I shall show you what is roaring in your well. I will make it come out and you will be able to kill it."

Whereupon the village menfolk take up their spears and clubs and follow Kalulu to the stream. There, as pre-arranged with Kalulu, they lurk round the edge of the water hole and wait.

Kalulu then begins to chat with Nkhala who, in the course of their conversation, comes out of the well.

"How then do you scare the villagers?" Kalulu asks his fellow animal.

Nkhala replies: "I go –
(Singing:)
N: Hu-uuu! There's a village
A: *Yaya lero kumangalengale*
N: Hu-uuu! that abused me
A: *Yaya lero kumangalengale*
N: Hu-uuu! at their millet
A: *Yaya lero kumangalengale*
N: Hu-uuu!
(NARRATOR speaks rapidly:)
Then the men leap out of their hiding places and crush Nkhala to a pulp. I have concluded [the tale].

6. The Unmarried Brother

This tale was performed in the sitting room of my house at Phwezi Secondary School at around mid-afternoon. Nyaviyuyi's audience was made up of the author and six girls, all children of teachers at Phwezi. She sat on a palm carpet, the tape recorder placed on a stool before her. Her audience sat about her around the tape recorder.

Guide to Idiophone Sounds

thibu!: th as th in Thames (river); *i* as i
   in tip; *bu* as boo in boot.
ẇeyu: ẇe as ve in venue (but with a weak
   v); *yu* as in you.
kwiti: kwi as quee in queen; *ti* as in tea
mbikitu!: mbi as mbi in ambition; *ki* as ki
   in kit; *tu* as in to
yii!: as yea in yeast
akee: a as in ah; *kee* as ca in cake.
zukuu!: zu as in zoo; *kuu* as in coo

(Nyaviyuyi was jovial throughout this performance)

THE SONS of a certain woman and a certain man were four in number. Three were married, the fourth was unmarried.

One day all the four of them went to the bush to hunt. They killed a reed buck.

Returning home from the hunt, they stopped not too far from their village, so as to skin and gut their kill. Having cut up the reed buck, and having shared out the meat among themselves, they now say to each other: "Let's call women to come and carry the meat home. Who will be the first to call?"

Then they begin to taunt their unmarried brother:

(NARRATOR speaks in mocking tones:)

"Who else should be the first to call but the one that is unmarried? He that has no house should start calling, for he has to bother his mother to come for the meat. And we have to grant old women the honour of always coming first in the queue!"

And all the three laugh spitefully.

Then the unmarried brother begins to call:

(NARRATOR leads the singing in humble tones:)

NARRATOR: Mother of mine, mother of mine

AUDIENCE: *Zandile*

N: Come and receive
A: *Zandile*
N: This piece of meat
A: *Zandile*
N: Nothing we bring*
A: *Zandile*
N: It's a piece of buck
A: *Zandile*

His mother comes and receives the meat. Now the married brothers begin to call. The first one goes –

(NARRATOR leads the singing in tones showing great pride:)
N: Wife of mine, wife of mine
A: *Zandile*
N: Wife of mine, wife of mine
A: *Zandile*
N: Come and receive
A: *Zandile*
N: This piece of meat
A: *Zandile*
N: Nothing we bring
A: *Zandile*
N: It's a piece of buck
A: *Zandile*

His wife comes and receives the meat.

The second one also calls:
(Singing:)
N: Wife of mine, wife of mine
A: *Zandile....*

His wife comes to receive the meat.

Now the third brother brings up the rear:
(Singing:)
N: Wife of mine, wife of mine

A: *Zandile...*

His wife comes for the meat

Then they all make their way to the village.

The next day they again go out to the forest for a hunt. But this time the unmarried brother declines to go with the other three. He decides to spend the day in the village.

Then he obtains the trunk of a *chipombola* tree and carves it...
(NARRATOR mimes the thorough tenderness with which the carving is being fashioned with gentle, caressing gestures of her hands, mentioning the word for carve at each gesture) ...into the form of a very beautiful young woman. He adorns the carved woman with *mphande* beads – one *mphande* on the head, a *mphande* around each knee, each wrist and each ankle.

(NARRATOR breaks into shrill tones of praise:)
Talk of beauty – the adorned carving is a real beauty!

He places the carving in his hut. The following day, off he goes with his brothers for a hunt in the forest. They happen to kill a reed buck again. And then, reaching the place where they customarily skin and gut their kills, they stop over and cut up that reed buck of theirs.

Having cut up their beast, the three brothers begin to tease their younger brother in the usual manner.

---

* It's not uncommon for hunters to belittle their success in the hunt.

43

(NARRATOR speaks in taunt-
ing tones:)

"Now it's time to call the women. And of course the unmarried one had better start off the calling! Then they laugh their friend to scorn.

Their contemptuous laugher becomes even louder when they hear what their younger brother says as he begins to call. For he is saying:

(NARRATOR leads the singing
in proud tones:)

N: Wife of mine, wife of mine

A: *Zandile*

N: Wife of mine, wife of mine

A: *Zandile*

N: Come and receive

A: *Zandile*

N: This piece of meat

A: *Zandile*

N: Nothing we bring

A: *Zandile*

N: It's a piece of buck

A: *Zandile*

(NARRATOR breaks into
exclamatory tones:)

There comes the exceedingly beautiful wife of the younger brother!...

(NARRATOR's face beams as
she shrieks in cadences of rising
excitement the following idio-
phones for radiance, a delicate
flourishing of the hand accom-
panying each idiophone:)
Thibu! Thibu-thibu! Ŵeyu-ŵeyu-
ŵeyu-ŵeyu-ŵeyu-ŵeyu!

The other three brothers are stunned by such surpassing beauty and they all bow *kwiti-kwiti-kwiti*
(NARRATOR bows low at the
idiophone kwiti-kwiti-kwiti)
before the approaching radiance.

Then the beauty arrives, receives the meat from her man, and off she goes.

With noticeable lack of enthusiasm now, the three elder brothers, one after another, call their wives:

(NARRATOR leads the singing
in a feeble voice:)

N: Wife of mine, wife of mine

A: *Zandile....*

One after another their wives come and receive the meat.

Well, so far so good. The next day all the four of them again go off into the bush to hunt.

Meanwhile, the local chief has heard about it all; people have reported to him, saying:

(NARRATOR speaks in shrill
tones:)

"She's such a beauty! You should see her, O chief!"

The chief comes and takes just one look at the young lady. Then he says:
(In a smug tone of voice):

"Does this beauty fit that young man? Certainly not!" With that, he abducts her *mbikitu!*
(At the idiophone mbikitu!
NARRATOR mimes the action of
snatching something)
– taking her to his compound.

Those four brothers return from their hunt. They arrive at the usual skinning and gutting place. There they cut up the reed buck they have killed, and share out the meat among

44

themselves.

The three elder brothers then say to the youngest:

(NARRATOR speaks in sub-dued tones:)

"Go on. Call."

The young brother calls:

(Singing:)

N: Wife of mine, wife of mine
A: *Zandile*
N: Wife of mine, wife of mine)
A: *Zandile*
N: Come and receive
A: *Zandile*
N: This piece of meat
A: *Zandile*
N: Nothing we bring
A: *Zandile*
N: It's a piece of buck
A: *Zandile*

(NARRATOR speaks in a voice of bewilderment:)

Yii! – no response.

The other brothers then call in the same manner. Their wives show up and receive the meat.

When the younger brother eventually hears that his wife has been abducted by the chief, he thinks long and hard as to whom he might send to the chief. He tries one bird after another. Not one proves a suitable messenger.

In the end a wood pigeon appears on the scene. He decides to try it. He tells it:

(NARRATOR speaks in a pregnantly calm voice:)

"Go and tell the chief to return to me the *mphande* the lady is wearing around her ankles."

Wood Pigeon duly flies to the chief's house and there sings before him:

(NARRATOR leads the singing in admonitory tones:)

N: *Chakum'potola kuku*
A: *Chakum'potola*
N: Send back through me the ankle *mphande*
A: *Chakum'potola*

The chief says,

(NARRATOR speaks in a dismissive tone of voice:)

"*Akee!* – tu! tut! What are two miserable *mphande* compared with the surpassing beauty of this lady?" With that he quickly plucks off the ankle *mphande*. And Wood Pigeon returns them to the younger brother. Then the young man sends Wood Pigeon back to the chief.

(NARRATOR speaks with the same pregnant calmness:)

"Go and bring me the *mphande* she is wearing around her knees."

Wood Pigeon dutifully returns to the chief, and there sings:

(Singing:)

N: *Chakum'potola kuku*
A: *Chakum'potola*
N: Send back through me the knee *mphande*
A: *Chukum'potola*

The chief thinks nothing of pulling the *mphande* from around the lady's knees and returning them to the young man.

Wood Pigeon is next sent to bring back the *mphande* from the wrists. And the chief readily complies. Then the young man dispatch-

es Wood Pigeon to the chief with
the final demand:

*(NARRATOR now speaks with
a calmness that is almost glee-
ful:)*

"Bring me the *mphande* the lady
is wearing on her head."

Wood Pigeon once again alights
before the chief. It sings:

(Singing:)

N: *Chakum'potola kuku*

A: *Chakum'potola*

N: Send back through me the head
mphande

A: *Chakum'potola*

The chief says, *"Akee-akee* −
what of it?" But no sooner does he
pluck the *mphande* off the lady's
head than a chipombola tree materi-
alizes *zukuu!* before him.

*(At the idiophone zukuu!
NARRATOR mimes with out-
stretched arms the outline of
a shady tree. Then she speaks
with mocking relish:)*

The woman has turned back into a
tree! The chief has failed in his evil
designs! End of tale.

7. The Wife and the Delicious Eggs

This tale was performed in the sitting room of my house at Phwezi Secondary School at around mid-afternoon. Nyaviyuyi's audience consisted of the author, one woman (Nyaviyuyi's half-sister) and nine children, three of them Nyaviyuyi had brought along from her nearby village and the rest children of teachers at Phwezi. Nyaviyuyi sat in an arm-chair (as did her sister), the tape recorder placed on the coffee table before her. The children sat on the floor.

Guide to Idiophone Sounds

lililili!: li as lea in lean.

kokaa!: as coca in coca cola with a long final a.

kha!: as kha in khaki.

keŵe!: ke as ke in kept; ŵe as ve in venue (but with a weak v).

kusu: ku as in coo; su as soo in soon

(The general gaiety of this performance was tempered with a touch of sombreness)

A BAND of men went for a hunt in the forest. Now, as they hunted, they stumbled upon an unusually huge clutch of eggs.

Being racked with hunger at the time, those men began to crack and suck the eggs, saying,

(NARRATOR speaks in exclamatory tones:)

"Ah! What delicious things!"

They sucked to their satisfaction — and yet the immense clutch looked still intact.

Those men liked the eggs so much that they agreed to come for a suck at the clutch each time they were in the forest on a hunt.

(In admonitory tones:)

But they further agreed that no other person should know about those mysterious eggs, and that not a single egg should be carried home by any of them

(In grimly derisive tones:)

Ah, despite this agreement, one of them conceals on himself a few of the eggs!

Back in the village that evening, the uncomplying man takes the eggs and gives them to his wife. The wife quickly consumes them with great relish.

Having tasted the palatable eggs, the wife says:

(In fawning tones:)

"What delicious things, dear husband! Do take me where they are found, so that I can be going there every day."

(NARRATOR grunts while shrugging her shoulders, miming the husband's alarm at the very thought of

47

doing what his wife is suggesting:)

"Hm! Hm! Hm!" says the husband. "Doing that sort of thing has been expressly forbidden by my colleagues."

(In ingratiating tones:)

"Oh please, do take me there," the wife insists. The husband:

(In a sing-song, self-justifying voice:)

"Oh well, it's no less a person than my wife who would like to be taken to the eggs...." Off they go. *(WOMAN in the audience interposes with the comment: "The obligations of marriage!"*)* They arrive at the clutch. They begin sucking the eggs right away. But, unlike his wife, the husband stands at a distance from the eggs – about that far *(NARRATOR points out the equivalent distance). (NARRATOR speaks in ominous tones:)*

Then the owner of the eggs launches itself somewhere in the distance! The husband notices the feathered giant's far reaching shadow. He warns his wife, saying:

(NARRATOR leads the singing in a pleading tone of voice:)

NARRATOR: Look my poor dear!

AUDIENCE*: Chidyamtambo walilima, Chidya-mtambo*

N: Look, my poor dear!

A: *Chidyamtambo walilima, Chi-dyamtambo*

N: There comes the owner!

A: *Chidyamtambo walilima, Chi-dyamtambo*
(NARRATOR speaks in tones of derision:)

No response from the wife! Only
—

(NARRATOR leads the singing in smug tones:)

N: Crack! Delicious!

A: *Chidyamtambo walilima, Chi-dyamtambo*

N: Crack! So delicious!

A: *Chidyamtambo walilima, Chi-dyamtambo*
(NARRATOR speaks in ominous tones:)

Aah, there the giant bird comes, advancing purposefully. Mm!

None the less, the wife is intently absorbed.

The husband calls out his warning:

(Singing:)

N: Look, my poor dear!

A: *Chidyamtambo walililima, Chi-dyamtambo*

N: Look, my poor dear!

A: *Chidyamtambo walilima, Chi-dyamtambo*

N: There comes the owner!

A: *Chidyamtambo walilima, Chi-dyamtambo*
(NARRATOR speaks with derision:)

The woman simply goes –

---

*   It may be pertinent to mention here that this lady, Nyakamshati, who was a divorcee, had recently moved in with a man much older than herself, a move that was disapproved by all her relatives.

48

(Singing:)

N: Crack! Delicious!

A: *Chidyamtambo walilima, Chidyamtambo*

N: Crack! So delicious!

A: *Chidyamtambo walilima, Chidyamtambo*

(NARRATOR speaks in ominous tones:)

The giant bird approaches relentlessly, though still afar off. *Lililili!* it hurtles through the air with sound and fury. Its shadow is now quite dense. Nevertheless, ...

(NARRATOR executes a single hand-clap to indicate the utter hopelessness of the situation)

... the wife just can't pull herself away from those eggs. The husband bemoans it all, saying to himself, "Exactly what my colleagues advised against! What do I do now?"

The colossal bird still approaches, with furious commotion.

Husband:

(Singing:)

N: Look, my poor dear!

A: *Chidyamtambo walilima, Chidyamtambo*

N: Look, my poor dear!

A: *Chidyamtambo walilima, Chidyamtambo*

N: There comes the owner!

A: *Chidyamtambo walilima, Chidyamtambo*

Wife:

(Singing:)

N: Crack! Delicious!

A: *Chidyamtambo walilima, Chidyamtambo*

N: Crack! So delicious!

A: *Chidyamtambo walilima, Chidyamtambo*

(NARRATOR speaks with taunting relish:)

Then it arrives, alighting heavily – *kokaa!* It instantly kills the wife – *kha!*

The husband bolts *keŵe!*

(At the idiophone keŵe! NARRATOR rubs her palms together with one quick stroke, miming the husband's speedy flight)

– tearing homeward through the forest.

(In mocking tones:)

And so the wife lies there *kusu* – gorged with eggs but lifeless. End of tale.

THE TALES IN CHITUMBUKA

1. Ngoza na Mfumu Wake

ŴA-NGOZA ŵakatolana na mwanarumi uyo wakazgokanga nkharamu – iwo kwambura kumanya kuti ndimo waliri mwanarumi wawo.

Mbwenu ghara ŵatolerana, mwanarumi ngawakuwuka kuya ku thondo. Wali, "Dende – namupenja dende." ˙

Ku thondo mwanarumi yura kutu-kutu-kutu

(Pakuti kutu-kutu-kutu,
MWIMBI wakujisunkhunya
thupi na nkhongono)

wazgoka chinkharamu. Chambako kwimba, chili:

(MWIMBI wakurongozga sumu
na mazgu ghakujinotha, uku
wakujisunkhunya thupi mwaku-
sanguruka:)

MWIMBI: Ah-ha-ha sefu yize pano
ŴAZOMEREZGI: Ndombole ya matete, ndombole
M: A-ha-ha ŵa-Ngoza ŵali ku kaya
Ŵ: Ndombole ya matete, ndombole
M: A-ha-ha ŵadyera nyama pera
Ŵ: Ndombole ya matete, ndombole
M: A-ha-ha bwenkha ŵalikukana
Ŵ: Ndombole ya matete, ndombole
M: A-ha-ha aaa, haya we!
Ŵ: Ndombole ya matete, ndombole
M: A-ha-ha aaa, haya we!
Ŵ: Ndombole ya matete, ndombole

Mbwenu sefu iyo papo iyo! Chili nayo kha! Irye-irye-irye-irye-irye! Wasidako chigha pera. Kutu-kutu – wazgoka munthu. Akuyegha chigha chira tembe-tembe, akuya ku kaya

(Na tumazgu twa chimwemwe:)
"E! Tipokerere dende!" Muwoli wake wakumupokerera.

Mwanarumi wali,

(Na vimazgu vikomi vya pasi-pasi:)
"Nangusanga vyajiryera; nasorako chigha pera. Nati hee, namnyako ni mwaŵi wane." (Uku warya ndiyo!) Ŵakurya para makora ghene. Namachero –

(Na vimazgu vikomi:)
"A, ndaruta mwe. Nkhapenjengeko dende." Mbwenu wakuruta ku thondo. Kutu-kutu – wazgoka nkharamu. Wali:

M: A-ha-ha boli wize pano
Ŵ: Ndombole ya matete, ndombole
M: A-ha-ha ŵa-Ngoza ŵali ku kaya
Ŵ: Ndombole ya matete, ndombole
M: A-ha-ha ŵadyera nyama pera
Ŵ: Ndombole ya matete, ndombole
M: A-ha-ha bwenkha ŵalikukana
Ŵ: Ndombole ya matete, ndombole
M: A-ha-ha aaa, haya we!
Ŵ: Ndombole ya matete, ndombole
M: A-ha-ha aa, haya we!
Ŵ: Ndombole ya matete, ndombole

A, chakoma boli. Charya cheneko, nakusidako chigha pera. Kutu-kutu
– chazgoka munthu. Wakuyegha nyama yira, wakuya ku kaya.

Sono ŵa-Ngoza ŵamba kuzizwa. Ŵakuti,

(Na mazgu ghakudinginika:)
"Aaa, ŵafumu ŵane nyama izi ŵakuyeghako chigha chimoza-chimoza ni nyama uli? A, rekani tiwone." Namachero:
(Na vimazgu vikomi:)
"A, mwe ndaruta mwe. Dende likusuzga."

Ŵala ku thondo. Ŵa-Ngoza ŵali munyuma; ŵakwenda mwakugwegweta kuti ŵafumu ŵaŵo ŵangaŵawona. Ŵali,
(Namazgu ghakurongora kunweka:)
"Mhanya uno m'paka niwone umo ŵafumu ŵane ŵakuŵambila."
Ŵala ku thondo kula kutu-kutu, ŵazgoka chinkharamu. Ngoza wakulaŵiska. Ŵali.
M: A-ha-ha sefu yize pano
Ŵ: Ndombole ya matete, ndombole
M: A-ha-ha ŵa-Ngoza ŵali ku kaya
Ŵ: Ndombole ya matete, ndombole
M: A-ha-ha ŵadyera nyama pera
Ŵ: Ndombole ya matete, ndombole
M: A-ha-ha bwenkha ŵalikukana
Ŵ: Ndombole ya matete, ndombole
M: A-ha-ha aaa, haya we!
Ŵ: Ndombole ya matete, ndombole
M: A-ha-ha aaa, haya we!
Ŵ: Ndombole ya matete, ndombole
(Sumu ngayamala, MWIMBI wakuŵika tuminwe kusi kwa maso ghake nakuguzila pasi vikope, uku wakun'yotola maso nakung'ola mlomo – kulongola kuti vinthu vyatondeka)
Yii! Ŵayezgeso kwali kuchema:
M: A-ha-ha boli wize pano
Ŵ: Ndombole ya matete ndombole
M: A-ha-ha ŵa-Ngoza ŵali ku kaya
Ŵ: Ndombole ya matete, ndombole

M: A-ha-ha ŵadyera nyama pera
Ŵ: Ndombole ya matete, ndombole
M: A-ha-ha-ha bwenkha ŵalikukana
Ŵ: Ndombole ya matete, ndombole
M: A-ha-ha aaa, haya we!
Ŵ: Ndombole ya matete, ndombole
M: A-ha-ha aaa, haya we!
Ŵ: Ndombole ya matete, ndombole
(Na mazgu ghakuhoya:)
Nyama ong! Mbwenu ŵakuzgoka waka munthu.
Ngoza wali,
(Na mazgu ghachitenthe:)
"Hi! Ndimo ŵakuchitira ŵafumu ŵane!" Waliyegha m'paka pa kaya.
Wati wafika pa kaya, nga wakutola thuli nakuthamo ngoma. Ngawakuchema ŵanakazi ŵanyake wali,
(Na tumazgu twakuhenera)
"Mwe zaninge tipule katiki-tiki, nimusambizgeni kasumu kakupulira!"
Ŵakupula thi! thi! thi!
(Pa thi! waliyose, MWIMBI wakuyerezgera kupula)
Ngoza wakwimba wali:
M: A-ha-ha-ha sefu yize pano
Ŵ: Ndombole ya matete, ndombole
M: A-ha-ha boli wize pano
Ŵ: Ndombole ya matete, ndombole
M: A-ha-ha ŵa-Ngoza ŵali ku kaya
Ŵ: Ndombole ya matete, ndombole
M: A-ha-ha ŵadyera nyama pera
Ŵ: Ndombole ya matete, ndombole
M: A-ha-ha bwenkha ŵalikukana
Ŵ: Ndombole ya matete, ndombole
M: A-ha-ha aaa, haya we!
Ŵ: Ndombole ya matete, ndombole

M: A-ha-ha aaa, haya we!

Ŵ: Ndombole ya matete, ndombole

Mwanarumi wakwiza nthe uko, wakupulika kuti katiki-tiki wakonda pa kaya! Pakufika pafupi na muzi wasanga sumu iyo ŵakwimba pakupula ni sumu yake yakuŵambila. Mbwenu lusoko lwamumalira.

Ŵanakazi ŵali,

(Na tumazgu twakuhenera:)

"Eee, mwiza na kasumu kaweme chomene, ŵa-Ngoza!"

Mwanarumi yura ngawakukhara pasi musi mwachivwati. Wali,

(Na mazgu ghakudandawula:)

"Ŵawoli ŵane ŵangunijoŵerera mhanya uno. Ndicho chifukwa nyama zangukana kwiza. Kwamara – nitondekenge lero kukoma nyama."

Kute bii, ŵanthu ŵakupatukana – uyu m'nyumba yake, uyu yake.

M'nyumba ya ŵa-Ngoza mfumu wawo wali,

(Na mazgu ghakunyengerera:)

"Ŵawoli ŵane, kasumu kala mwapuliranga naŵanyinu nkhaweme chomene; ndipo kakwenerera chomene ise taŵachiŵinda. Mphanyi mwanimbirapo."

(Na mazgu gha wofi:)

"Hee, ŵafumu ŵane ŵapulikizganga ka?"

Ŵayezge kumeka-meka na kuteta utesi kuti kasumu ŵakaruwa, ŵafumu ŵawo ŵakaŵanyengerera ndipera, ŵali, "Yayi, imbanipo."

Ŵa-Ngoza ngaŵakwambako waka kwimba, ŵali,

(MWIMBI wakurongozga sumu na tumazgu twakusingo-singo, twa wofi:)

M: A-ha-ha-sefu yize pano

Ŵ: Ndombole ya matete, ndombole

M: A-ha-ha boli wize pano

Ŵ: Ndombole ya matete, ndombole

M: A-ha-ha ŵa-Ngoza ŵali ku kaya

Ŵ: Ndombole ya matete, ndombole

M: A-ha-ha ŵadyera nyama pera

Ŵ: Ndombole ya matete, ndombole

M: A-ha-ha bwenkha ŵali kukana

Ŵ: Ndombole ya matete, ndombole

M: A-ha-ha aaa, haya we!

Ŵ: Ndombole ya matete, ndombole

M: A-ha-ha aaa, haya we!

Ŵ: Ndombole ya matete, ndombole

Mwanarumi kutu-kutu – wazgoka nkharamu. Kanye-kanye ŵawoli ŵake. Ving'unu mbii! Chamara.

2. Maliro na Chipili

ŴANA ŵakaya ku dambo kuyakaskugha pa chiziŵa. Ŵakubila, ŵakubila, ŵakubila. Mbwenu yumoza, zina lake Maliro, waseka: Chipili chikutataŵa. Chili, *(MWIMBI wakukora kalezulezu uku wakumwemwetera na kuyowoya na mazgu ghakurongora kudokera:)* "A, mwana mino kutowa yura!"
Mbwenu chipili chila ngachikwamba kumuŵenda mwana yura. *(Na mazgu ghaluŵiro-luŵiro:)* Chamukora! Chamuguzira pasi pa maji! Ŵana ŵanyake ngaŵakuwerera ku kaya. Ŵakukati ku kaya kura, ŵakuti,
(Na tumazgu twa wanichi:) "A-Maliro nkhulije: Ŵatizgeŵa ŵaka pa maji."
Ŵanthu ŵakapenja chomene – Maliro wangawoneka yayi. Mbwenu ngaŵakwamba waka kulira nyifwa yake.
Sono dazi limoza, ŵanthu ŵakati ŵaleka nakuleka kulira nyifwa ya Maliro, mwana msepuka zina lake Mdangu wakafuma ku kaya: "Nkhateme matete...."
Akutema matete kha-kha, kha-kha
(Pa kha-kha waliyose MWIMBI wakuyerezgera kutema na phwitika) mumphepete mwa chiziŵa chira. Mbwenu ngaŵakupulika pa maji

pakwimba pakuti:
(MWIMBI wakurongozga kwimba sumu na mazgu ghakudinginika:)
MWIMBI: Ŵa-Mdangu mwizaso
ŴAZOMEREZGI: Mwiza, mwiza msesese
M: M'kaphare ku ŵamama
Ŵ: Mwiza, mwiza msesese
M: Ŵa-Maliro ŵali uku
Ŵ: Mwiza, mwiza msesese
M: Ŵakaŵakora pa maji
Ŵ: Mwiza, mwiza msesese
M: Chifukwa chake ni mino
Ŵ: Mwiza, mwiza msesese
Mdangu ngawakupokera wakuti:
M: Enya nadi
Ŵ: Dede
M: Ndayamukunena
Ŵ: Dede
M: Ku ŵanyoko ŵako
Ŵ: Dede
M: Ŵa-Maliro ŵali uku
Ŵ: Dede
M: Ŵakaŵakora pa maji
Ŵ: Dede
M: Chifukwa chake ni mino
Ŵ: Dede
Mbwenu Mdangu ngawakuwera. Akuphalira ŵalala akuti,
(Natumazgu twakurongora kuzizikika:)
"Imwe: Ndamnyinu ku dambo uku: Nkhuti niteme matete, mbwenu munthu wakwimba pa chiziŵa wakuti ŵa-Maliro ŵakaŵakora pa

maji chifukwa cha mino." Ŵalala ŵakuti,

(Na mazgu ghakurongora kususka:)
"Vichi? Walotanga kwali?"

Wali,

(Na tumazgu twa wanichi:)
"Nalotanga yayi. Rekani pera niwerereko nkhapulike makora."

Akuruta…. Matete kha-kha, kha-kha

(MWIMBI wakuyerezgera kutema na phwitika).

Pa chiziŵa payamba kwimba. Pali:

M: Ŵa-Mdangu mwizaso
Ŵ: Mwiza, mwiza musesese
M: M'kaphare ku ŵamama
Ŵ: Mwiza, mwiza musesese
M: Ŵa-Maliro ŵali uku
Ŵ: Mwiza, mwiza musesese
M: Ŵakaŵakora pa maji
Ŵ: Mwiza, mwiza msesese
M: Chifukwa chake ni mino
Ŵ: Mwiza, mwiza musesese

Mdangu wali:

M: Enya nadi
Ŵ: Dede
M: Ndayamukunena
Ŵ: Dede
M: Ku ŵanyoko ŵako
Ŵ: Dede
M: Ŵa-Maliro ŵali uku
Ŵ: Dede
M: Ŵakaŵakora pa maji
Ŵ: Dede
M: Chifukwa chake ni mino
Ŵ: Dede

Nadi wakuyakaphara kura. Sono ŵalala ŵakuti,

(Na mazgu ghakurongora kuzizikika:)

"A, uyu mwana tikapulike makora emwe."

Ŵapapi ŵa Maliro, na ŵalala ŵanyake, na mweneyuyu Mdangu ngaŵakuruta ku matete. Mdangu waŵaphalira kuti ŵimilire ŵapulikizgenge para iyo wakutema matete.

Akwambako kha-kha, kha-kha

(MWIMBI wakuyerezgera kutema na phwitika).

Mbwenu pa maji payamba kwimba

M: Ŵa-Mdangu mwizaso
Ŵ: Mwiza, mwiza msesese
M: M'kaphare ku ŵamama
Ŵ: Mwiza, mwiza msesese
M: Ŵa-Maliro ŵali uku
Ŵ: Mwiza, mwiza msesese
M: Ŵakaŵakora pa maji
Ŵ: Mwiza, mwiza msesese
M: Chifukwa chake ni mino
Ŵ: Mwiza, mwiza msesese

Akupokera Mdangu:

M: Enya nadi
Ŵ: Dede
M: Ndayamukunena
Ŵ: Dede
M: Ku ŵanyoko ŵako
Ŵ: Dede
M: Ŵa-Maliro ŵali uku
Ŵ: Dede
M: Ŵakaŵakora pa maji
Ŵ: Dede
M: Chifukwa chake ni mino
Ŵ: Dede

(Na mazgu ghakurongora kuzukuma:)

Hi! Ŵajipulikira ŵekha: Chipili chilikuyegha mwana wawo! Ŵakuwera ku kaya.

(Na mazgu ghakurongora

mwamphu ukuru:)

Penjani mboni zinandi, na salu yituŵa.Ŵafikaso pa chiziŵa para.

Ndiyo tolani salu yituŵa yira, na mboni zira ngaŵakuponya pa maji pa chipili para.

Ndiyo Maliro wuu, wali pa mtunda. Chamara.

3. Mwanakazi Uyo Wakazgokanga Munkhwere

MNYAMATA wakatola mwana-kazi. Wakachita kumsomphola. Wakamanya cha kuti mwanakazi yura wakaŵa na kaluso kakuzgoka munkhwere na kwiba vya ŵanthu. Wakarutanga ku thondo kwa yekha. Kula ngawakukazgoka munkhwere – mchila ndolololo.

(Pakuti ndolololo, mwana yumoza mkati mwa wumba wa ŵakutegherezga wakuseka).

Ngawakwiba vya ŵanthu ibe-ibe-ibe. Usange wiba wakhuta, mbwenu ngawakuguza mchila kwe! kuti udu-muke. Para mchila wadumuka mbwenu ngawakuzgoka munthu. Mbwenu wakuwera, akwiza ku kaya. Namachero napo ntheura pera: Akuruta ku thondo nakukaz-goka munkhwere. Irye-irye-irye vya ŵanthu. Sima pakaya akukana. Sono ŵanthu pa kaya ŵakwamba kuzizwa kuti: "Ka uyu akuryachi? A, ipo timjoŵerere uko wakwenda." Ŵakamjoŵerera. Waruta ku thondo kula akuzgoka munkhwere – ŵakumwona. Akwiba vya ŵanthu.

(Na mazgu ghakuhoya:)

Mwenekale waguze mchila kuti wazgoke munthu, watondeka – ka ŵanthu ŵamwona. Waguzire muno kwali – to!

(Na mazgu ghachitenthe:)

"Hekwi! Ndite uli ine apa mchila ukukana kudumuka?"

Ngawakuzetekuka kuya ku kaya.Akutola mbavi nakuwereraso ku thondo kuti wakadumure mchila. Ngawakukhara pa chisinga kuti wadumule makora mchila. Wadanga kwimba, wali:

(MWIMBI wakurongozga sumu na mazgu ghakurongora kuzingiziwa:)

MWIMBI: Wamchila wane dumu-ka, tila

ŴAZOMEREZGI: Tendengala tila

M: Mchila wane dumuka, tila

Ŵ: Tendengala tila

M: Umkolwe nge ngwane, tila

Ŵ: Tendengala tila

M: Uchizondu nge ngwane, tila

Ŵ: Tendengala tila

M: Junyunthu we hihi, ayo!

Ŵ: Tendengala tila

M: Junyunthu we hihi, ayo!

Ŵ: Tendengala tila

Mbavi yikujunyunthuka waka na kum'pweteka. Mchila ukukana kudumuka.

Wafuma para wakakhara pa chisinga chinyake. Wali:

M: Wamchila wane dumuka, tila

Ŵ: Tendengala tila

M: Dumuka, tila

Ŵ: Tendengala tila

M: Uchizondu nge ngwane, tila

Ŵ: Tendengala tila

M: Umkolwe nge ngwane, tila

Ŵ: Tendengala tila
M: Junyunthu we hihi, ayo!
Ŵ: Tendengala tila
M: Junyunthu we hihi, ayo!
Ŵ: Tendengala tila
(Sumu ngayamara, MWIMBI wakukuŵa mapi mwa luŵiro-luŵiro kaŵiri nakukwezga mawoko mchanya, ngati wadukenge – kurongora umo munkhwere yura wakadukira:)
Wali m'khuni m'chanya sala!, kuti panji m'khuni mchanya ndimo mchila ungakazomera kudumuka. Wakulimbana nakuti mchila nidumule, nizgoke munthu:
(Na mazgu ghakudinginika:)
"Nangutengwa makora kwa mfumu wane: Uchikhazi wanguŵa wane; ufumukazi pa nyumba wanguŵa wane."
M: Wamchila wane dumuka, tila
Ŵ: Tendengala, tila
M: Mchila wane dumuka, tila
Ŵ: Tendengala tila

M: Uchizondu nge ngwane, tila
Ŵ: Tendengala tila
M: Umkolwe nge ngwane, tila
Ŵ: Tendengala tila
M: Junyunthu we hihi ayo!
Ŵ: Tendengala, tila
M: Junyunthu we hihi ayo!
Ŵ: Tendengala tila
(Na mazgu ghakuseka:)
Mchila ungadumuka yayi.

Ŵala mbwenu ngaŵakurutirira kwiba vya ŵanthu.

Mbwenu munthu mnyake ngawakuŵathya: Akutola chingoma, akupayika m'khuni.

(Na mazgu ghakuhoya:)
Iwo nkhatole ngoma yira, mbwenu munthu yura wali na kamuvwi e!...
(Pakuti e!, MWIMBI wakupinkhula kamunwe, kurongora upusu uwo muvwi ukaponyekera)
Ŵafwa. Chamara.

4. Kasepuka na Chimilaŵanthu

KUKIZA chiyuni chikuru chomeni. Mafumu ghakafuma nkhu na nkhu, kuzura pha-pha-pha pa muzi wa fumu yikuru; ŵakati tikome kwali, ŵakatondeka.

Sono kasepuka zina lake Funkhamakhwelu ndiko kakuti,

(MWIMBI wakuyowoya na tumazgu tuchoko-tuchoko ndipo twakujiyuyura:)

"Ndiyezge nane."

Fumu yikuru yikati,

(Na mazgu ghaukali, ndiposo ghakunyoza:)

"Choka iwe! Ungayezga iwe apa, chinthu chakuti chatonda mafumu?"

Kweni mafumu ghanyake ghakati, "Rekani wayezge nayo."

Mafumu ghakalimbana, ghakalimbana. Mbwenu ngaŵakumuzomerezga.

Sono, apo wakuzakayezga para, kamuvwi phwililili,

(Pakuti phwililili, MWIMBI wakurongora kamunwe kuchanya, kuyerezgera umo muvwi ukathuvukira) ku chiyuni kula kweche! Mbwenu chiyuni kokoolololo.

(Pakuti kokoolololo, MWIMBI wakukupizga mawoko, kuyerezgera umo chiyuni chikapozomokera chikati chalasika na kukomeka) (Fumu yikuru yikayowoya kuti "Usange wati wakome chiyuni ichi pera, nitimulekerenge ufumu wa charu ichi"). Ŵanthu ŵali, "Mwawona, wakoma mnyinu. Mute uli?"

Fumu yikuru yikati,

(Na mazgu ghakunyoza:)

"Aaa, ipo wakome Munkhokoko." Mbwenu ngakakuponya muvwi kuchanya! Munkhokoko lililili!

(Pakuti lililili, MWIMBI wakukupizga mawoko kuyerezgera umo Huŵa yikapozomokera kufuma kuchanya yikati yalasika na kukomeka) Fumu yikuru yikati, "Aaa, Jiwundembo wakumala ŵanthu. Ipo ndiko warute, wakakome."

Ndimo Funkhamakhwelu wakarutira kwa Jiwundembo. Wakayegha mchere na ncheŵe zake zinkhonde: Nkharamu, Nthoromi, Makokota, Chimthiko na Nyerenjani.

Kukafika pa Jiwundembo, wakamnozgera malo nayo pamphepete para.

Sono na usiku Jiwundembo wakuti "Nyama sono yagona; niyikome nirye."

Ghala wakuti chijino chake ng'we

(Pakuti ng'we! MWIMBI wakuŵika kamunwe ku mlomo wake, kuyerezgera kuti kamunwe ndiko nchijino chitali) kuti nimkang'anthe, Funkhama-

khwelu mchere pa moto wa!
(Na vimazgu viheni-viheni vya besi:)
"Hrruu! Vivichi vikuphwaraphwatuka pa moto?"
Funkhamakhwelu wali,
(Na tumazgu tuchoko-tuchoko)
"Manyi."
Mbwenu usange chati chijino ng'we! kuti chimkang'anthe, Funkhamakhwelu mchere pa moto wa! Jiwundembo wakatondeka kukoma Funkhamakhwelu usiku ula.

Sono kukucha ngwe namachero, Jiwundembo wali "Munthu uyu wanitonda usiku. Nimughanaghanire nthowa yinyake."

Wazakati busu [mavi] m'khuni m'chanya mbwi! Membe wa-wa-wa. Wakuwera kula wakuti kwa Funkhamakhwelu,
(Na mazgu ghakunyengerera)
"Kanipakulire njuchi zili mu khuni la nyamthwewo mula."
Funkamakhwelu wakazomera. Wakaruta na ncheŵe yimoza pera: Nkharamu. Wakakwera khuni lira m'chanya.

Cha-Jiwundembo luŵiro chikamronda, nakwamba kutema khuni lira:
(MWIMBI wakwambako kwimba na vimazgu vyakofya. Pa go! waliyose, MWIMBI wakuyerezgera kutema na chimbavi chikuru:)
MWIMBI: Chati go!
ŴAZOMEREZGI: Waliwa lero, waliwa

M: Chati go!
Ŵ: Waliwa lero, waliwa
M: Chati go!
Ŵ: Waliwa lero, waliwa
(Na mazgu ghaluŵiro-luŵiro:)
Khuni lite thenyu!, Munthyenkhu wakuti, "Nyamthwewo, wa khuni, ungawanga yayi: Wakakupanda ni Jiwundembo chara, wakakupanda ni Chiuta!" Mbwenu khuni lira siki-siki.

(Pakuti siki-siki, MWIMBI wakuwuskira m'chanya wawoko nakusunkhunya thupi lake, kurongora kukhora uko khuni likakhoraso)
Funkhamakhwelu sono wakwamba kuchema ncheŵe zake izo wakazisida kunyuma. Wali:
(MWIMBI wakurongozga kwimba na mazgu gha chitima, uku wakusunkhunya thupi kurongora usokwano:)
M: ŴaMakokota, yalira
Ŵ: Hee yalira
M: Na Nyerenjani, yalira
Ŵ: Hee yalira
M: Ine ndifwenge, yalira
Ŵ: Hee yalira
Mbwenu chikwambaso:
M: Chati go!
Ŵ: Waliwa lero, waliwa
M: Chati go!
Ŵ: Waliwa lero waliwa
M: Chati go!
Ŵ: Waliwa lero, waliwa
(Na mazgu ghaluŵiro-luŵiro:)
Khuni lite phi! Munthenkhu wakuti, "Nyamthewo akakupanda ni Chiuta: Khazikika!" Khuni siki-siki.

(Mwanakazi mkati mu wumba wa ŵakutegherezga wali "Vidokoni utesi!")

Ndipo wakuti

M: Ŵa Chimthiko, yalira

Ŵ: Hee yalira

M: Na Nyerenjani, yalira

Ŵ: Hee yalira

M: Ine ndifwenge, yalira

Ŵ: Hee yalira

Mbwenu. Kwakhara ncheŵe yake yimoza.

Chikwambaso kutema khuni:

M: Chati go!

Ŵ: Waliwa lero, waliwa

M: Chati go!

Ŵ: Waliwa lero, waliwa

M: Chati go!

Ŵ: Waliwa lero, waliwa

(Na mazgu ghaluŵiro-luŵiro:)

Khuni lite phi! Munthyenkhu wakuti, "Nyamthwewo wakakupanda ni Chiuta!"

Wali:

M: Mwe ŵaNthoromi, yalira

Ŵ: Hee yalira

M: Na Nyerenjani, yalira

Ŵ: Hee yalira

M: Ine ndifwenge, yalira

Ŵ: Hee yalira

Mbwenu. Ncheŵe zake zose zafika para jenjerere.

(Pakuti jenjerere, MWIMBI wakutambazura mawoko, kurongora umo ncheŵe zikayimira, uku wapanga mankhwinya pamaso kurongora umo ncheŵe zikakalipira)

Mbwenu wakuti, "Aaa. Sono ndipo." Watukusa kamuvwi para. Mwa Jiwundembo thi!

(Pakuti thi! MWIMBI wakujigwaza na kamunwe mu mbambo)

A-Jiwundembo kang'aa!

(Pakuti kang'aa! MWIMBI wakutambazura mawoko kurongora umo Chimilaŵanthu chikawira chagada chikati chalasika na kukomeka)

Fwamphulani! Ŵanyamata, ŵachekuru, ŵamwali: Nchi-nchi-nchi!

(Pakuti nchi-nchi-nchi! MWIMBI wakutambazura mawoko nakughendeska uku na uku, kurongora ukuru wa wumba wa ŵanthu awo ŵakafuma mu chinthumbo cha Jiwundembo)

Ŵanthu ŵala ŵakuchita kumuyegha m'chanya Funkhamakhwelu, ŵakurazga nayo ku muzi wa fumu yikuru. Iyo mwenecho wakwendakajihaya, wali:

(MWIMBI wakurongozga kwimba na kukondwa kukuru, uku wakusukhunya nthupi nga nipara wakuvina:)

M: Kabayi Muyune

Ŵ: Hee nyamalimba tema

M: Ndaruta ndabaya

Ŵ: Hee nyamalimba tema

M: Kabayi Munkhokoko

Ŵ: Hee nyamalimba tema

M: Ndaruta ndabaya

Ŵ: Hee nyamalimba tema

M: Kabayi Jiwundembo

Ŵ: Hee nyamalimba tema

M: Ndaruta ndabaya

Ŵ: Hee nyamalimba tema

Ŵanthu pa muzi wa fumu yikuru ula ŵakupulika kwimba kwa Funkhamakhwelu wachali kwiza kutali. Fumu yikuru ngayikulangura kuti dindi lijimike, dongo ŵabise pafupi. Nadi dindi lika-jimika, ndipo ŵakatandikapo mphasa.

Ŵanthu ŵala ŵati ŵafika nayo mu muzi ula Funkhamakhwelu, fumu yikuru yikayowoya mwa upusikizgi kuti Funkhamakhwelu wakupokerereka mwa nchindi, ndipo yikamuphalira kuti wakhare pa mphasa kuti wavwarikike mphumphu ya ufumu.

Funkhamakhwelu wati nikhare, mbwenu ng'onomo – wawa mu dindi! Mbwenu ŵakwiza wunde-wunde.

Ŵanthu ŵala ŵakafuma mu nthumbo ya Jiwundembo ŵenecho-kaya ŵakwiza gaŵane-gaŵane. Kuli "Ine ŵane aŵa! Ine aŵa!"

(Na mazgu ghakofya:)

Ncheŵe jenjerere. Kang'anthani ŵenecho-kaya! Kang'anthani! Upfu!   '

(Pakuti upfu! MWIMBI waku-phyera pa mlomo na kawoko, kurongora kuti pakaŵavye uyo wakapona ku ncheŵe zira)

Wiskewo-kuru yiku-yiku....

(Pakuti yiku-yiku, MWIMBI wakuyerezgera kuzgura chinthu icho chawundika)

– pa mtunda.

(Na mazgu ghakuhenera:)

Funkhamakhwelu   akapoka charu. Chamara.

5. Nkhala na Muzi

NKHALA yikafika apo mwanakazi akapwanthanga malezi. Yikati yafika para yikimilira nthe apo, nakulawilira mwanakazi yura akupeta malezi ghake.

Tuyuni twakupambana-pambana tukadekanga pa mwelero para, ndipo mwanakazi yura akatuŵinganga fyaa! kuti tungamba kurya malezi ghake

Yikati yalaŵilira, Nkhala yira yikawuka nakudumula pa mwelero para kuti yirutenge ku nyumba yake ku dambo.

Mwanakazi yura wakayiwona yikukwakwatuka pa mwelero. Ngawakulekezga kupeta malezi; akutola kakhuni nakuyiŵininkhura.

Wali,

(MWIMBI wakumweyula, kurongora thinkhu, uku nakawoko wakuyerezgera kupinkhura:)

"Fumanipo apa! Hakwe! Na a-Nkhala wuwo!"

Nkhala yikakwiya chomeni pakuŵininkhurika mwantheura. Icho chikayikwiyiskaso chomeni ni mazgu gha msunjiro ghakuti 'Na a-Nkhala wuwo!': "Chifukwa uli mwanakazi yura tuyuni wakatuyowoyera ntheura chara apo wakatuŵinganga?"

Yikati yafika ku dambo kula, Nkhala yikaghanaghana chomeni umo yingalangira ŵanthu ŵa muzi

ula chifukwa cha msunjiro uwo mwanakazi yura wakayichitira. Yili "Ninjire pa chisimi apo ŵakumwa maji."

Ŵanakazi pakuti ŵize ku chisimi ŵateke maji, mbwenu ngaŵakupulika chinthu chikuwuruma pa chisimi chikuti:

(Pa 'Hu-uuu! waliyose, MWIMBI wakukhotama – uku watukumura matama – na kuwuruma:)

MWIMBI: Hu-uuu! Ŵanthu ŵala

ŴAZOMEREZGI: Yaya lero kumangalengale

M: Hu-uuu! ŵakan'tukanga

Ŵ: Yaya lero kumangalengale

M: Hu-uuu! pa malezi ghawo

Ŵ: Yaya lero kumangalengale

M: Hu-uuu!

Ŵanakazi ŵala ŵakofyeka chomeni, ndipo ŵakachimbirira ku kaya na misuko ya mwazi. Ŵakapharira ŵanarumi pa kaya. Ŵanarumi ŵali,

(Na mazgu ghakurongora kususka:)

"Pali chinthu wuli pa chisimi? Tiyeni tikapulike."

Ŵanakazi ŵala ŵakarutaso ku chisimi, pamoza na ŵanarumi.

Mwanakazi yumoza wakuti wayezge kuteka maji, mbwenu kuwuruma uko pa chisimi:

M: Hu-uuu! Ŵanthu ŵala

Ŵ: Yaya lero kumangalengale

M: Hu-uuu! ŵakan'tukanga

Ŵ: Yaya lero kumangalengale

M: Hu-uuu! pa mwelero wawo
Ŵ: Yaya lero kumangalengale
M: Hu-uuu!

(Sumu ngayamara, MWIMBI wakukuŵa mapi mwaluŵiro-luŵiro kaŵiri, kurongora 'pachepa malo')

Ŵanthu wose ŵala ŵakachimbirira ku kaya na wofi ukuru.

(Na mazgu ghakuhoya:)
Muzi ula ukayungwa chomeni chifukwa cha maji. Ŵanthu mahara ghakamara; ŵakamanya chara chakuti ŵachite.

Sono dazi limoza, muzi uchali kulagha na maji, kukiza Kalulu. Ŵanthu ngaŵakumwandulira icho chaŵawira pa muzi ula.

Kalulu wali "Nditiyezge kumovwirani."

Kalulu wakaruta pa chisimi para ndipo wakamba kudumbiskana na Nkhala. Nkhala yili,

(Na mazgu ghakufinga:)
"Ŵanthu ŵala ŵakanichimbizga mwa msunjiro chomene pa mwelero wawo. Ŵacherwenge!"

Wakati wamara kudumbiskana na Nkhala, Kalulu wakarutaso ku muzi ula. Wali,

(Na mazgu ghakujiŵikamo:)
"Ndirondezgani mwaŵanthu, nkhamurongorani chinthu icho chikuwuruma pa chisimi chinu. Mwamkuchikoma."

Ŵanarumi ŵakatola nthonga na mikondo, ŵakaruta na Kalulu.

Kalulu wali, " Bisamani pafupi na chisimi." Ŵakabisama.

Kalulu wakamba kudumba na Nkhala. Ndipo Nkhala yikati yafumira pawalo pa chisimi, Kalulu wakayifumba kuti, "Sono ŵanthu ukuwofya uli?"

Nkhala yili, "Nkhuwuruma nkhuti:
M: Hu-uuu! Ŵanthu ŵala
Ŵ: Yaya lero kumangalengale
M: Hu-uuu! ŵakan'tukanga
Ŵ: Yaya lero kumangalengale
M: Hu-uuu! pa mwelero wawo
Ŵ: Yaya lero kumangalengale
M: Hu-uuu!

(Na mazgu ghaluŵiro-luŵiro:)
Mbwenu ŵanthu ŵali nayo nkhala yira kome-kome. Namara.

6. Mnyamata Wambura Kutola

ŴANA ŵa mwanakazi na mwanarumi uyu ŵakaŵa ŵanayi. Ŵatatu ŵakaŵa ŵakutola, wachinayi wakaŵa wambura kutola.

Dazi limoza wose ŵanayi ŵakaruta ku thondo kukaŵamba nyama. Ku chisokole kula ŵakakomako mphato [mbaŵala].

Ŵakuwera kula ŵakimilira mu thondo pafupi na chikaya chawo, kuti ŵahembe nyama yawo.

Ŵati ŵadumula-dumula nyama yira, mbwenu ŵakuti, "Sono ticheme ŵanakazi ŵazakayegha nyama.

(MWIMBI wakutola mazgu ghakunyoza:)

"Ŵadange kuchema ni aŵa ŵambura kutola: Ka ŵalije nyumba; ŵazamuŵatolera mbanyinawo! Ŵachekuru nyengo zose tikwenera kuŵapa nchindi pakuŵaŵika ŵakwamba!" Ŵatatu ŵakutola ŵala ŵakaseka chimwazga-mtima.

Mbwenu wamumphara yura ngawakwamba kuchema. Wali:

(MWIMBI wakurongozga sumu na mazgu ghakujiyuyura:)

MWIMBI: Ŵamama   ŵane, ŵamama

ŴAZOMEREZGA: Zandile

M: Ŵamama ŵane, ŵamama

Ŵ: Zandile

M: Zani mupoke

Ŵ: Zandile

M: Nyama yino

Ŵ: Zandile

M: Tawera waka

Ŵ: Zandile

M: Nyama ni mphato

Ŵ: Zandile

Ŵakwiza anyina ŵakuzakapoka. Ŵambako kuchema ŵakutola sono.

Wakwamba wali:

(MWIMBI wakurongozga sumu na mazgu ghakujinotha:)

M: Ŵawoli ŵane, ŵawoli

Ŵ: Zandile

M: Ŵawoli ŵane, ŵawoli

Ŵ: Zandile

M: Zani mupoke

Ŵ: Zandile

M: Nyama yino

Ŵ: Zandile

M: Tawera waka

Ŵ: Zandile

M: Nyama ni mphato

Ŵ: Zandile

Ŵakuzakapoka.

Wachiŵiri nayo wakuchema:

M: Ŵawoli ŵane, ŵawoli

Ŵ: Zandile...

Ŵakuzakapoka.

Sono wakumalizga wachitatu:

M: Ŵawoli ŵane, ŵawoli

Ŵ: Zandile....

Ŵakuzakapoka.

Mbwenu ŵakuwera ŵakuya ku kaya.

Namachero ŵakufumaso; ŵakuruta ku chisokole. Wambura kutola

yura wakana kuyako; ŵaruta ŵatatu pera ŵala. Iyo watandara pa kaya.

Mbwenu waŵaja chipombola chake ŵaje-ŵaje-ŵaje.

(Pa 'ŵaje' waliyose, MWIMBI wakusunkhunya kawoko makora-makora, kurongora umo mnyamata wakupwerererera pakuŵaja)

Wachiŵaja kuti chiwoneke kanakazi kakutowa chomene. Wachivwarika na mphande wuwo – yinyake pa mutu, yinyake mu makongono, yinyake mu mawoko, yinyake ku vitende:

(MWIMBI wakuhaya na mazgu gha pachanya:)

Thonyi, thonyi nadi!

Mbwenu. Wachiŵika mu mphara yake.

Namachero mnyamata yura ngawakuruta nawo ŵakuru ŵake ku chisokole. Ngaŵakukomaso mphato.

Mbwenu ŵatiŵafika para ŵakuhembera nyama zawo madazi ghose ngaŵakukhara pasi nakutumbula mphato yira. Ŵatiŵamara kudumula nyama, ŵakuru ŵake ŵali,

(Na mazgu ghakunyoza:)

"Ticheme ŵanakazi sono. Kweni ŵadange kuchema ni aŵa namwe, ŵambura kutola." Ngaŵakumseka chimwazga-mtima mnyawo.

Seko zawo zikurutirira apo ŵakupulika kuti mnyawo pakuchema wakuti:

(MWIMBI wakurongozga sumu na mazgu ghakujinotha:)

M: Ŵawoli ŵane, ŵawoli

Ŵ: Zandile

M: Ŵawoli ŵane, ŵawoli

Ŵ: Zandile

M: Zani mupoke

Ŵ: Zandile

M: Nyama yino

Ŵ: Zandile

M: Tawela waka

Ŵ: Zandile

M: Nyama ni mphato

Ŵ: Zandile

(MWIMBI wakuchita kuchemerezga pakuyowoya:)

Kakufuma kula kanakazi:Thibu! thibu-thibu! Ŵeyu-ŵeyu-ŵeyu-ŵeyu-ŵeyu! Ŵakuru ŵake wose mbwenu kwiti-kwiti-kwiti*!*

(Pakuti kwiti-kwiti-kwiti!, MWIMBI wakusindama)

Kakwiza para; kakupoka nyama; kakuruta.

Mbwenu ŵakuru ŵake nawo ŵakuchema mwakugongowa. Ŵali:

(MWIMBI wakurongozga sumu na mazgu ghakusingo-singo:)

M: Ŵawoli ŵane, ŵawoli

Ŵ: Zandile…

Ŵawoli ŵawo ŵakuzakapoka.

Mbwenu na. Namachero ghake ngaŵakurutaso kuchisokole wose ŵanayi.

Fumu yapulika; ŵayiphalira ŵanthu kuti

(MWIMBI wakuyowoya na njeza zikuru:)

"Yayi, kuli mwanakazi uyo! Murute, afumu, mukamuwone."

Fumu yikwizakamuwona. Yikuti,

(Na mazgu gha msunjiro:)
"A, wakumwenerera uyu? Waku-
mwenerera yayi." Yili nayo mbikitu!
*(Pakuti mbikitu!, MWIMBI
wakuyerezgera kukwapula
chinthu na kawoko)*
Yaruta nayo ku nyumba zake.
Ŵanayi ŵala ngaŵakuwerako ku
chisokole. Ŵafika pa malo ghaku-
tumbulira nyama para. Ŵahemba
nyama, ŵadumula-dumula, ŵaga-
ŵana.Ŵakuru ŵake ŵali,
(Na mazgu ghakudonda-donda:)
"Chemanga."
Munung'una wali:
M: Ŵawoli ŵane, ŵawoli
Ŵ: Zandile
M: Ŵawoli ŵane, ŵawoli
Ŵ: Zandile
M: Zani mupoke
Ŵ: Zandile
M: Nyama yino
Ŵ: Zandile
M: Tawera waka
Ŵ: Zandile
M: Nyama ni mphato
Ŵ: Zandile
*(Na mazgu ghakurongora
kuzizikika:)*
Yii!
Ŵakuru ŵake nawo ŵaku-
chema. Ŵakwizakapoka nyama
ŵawoli ŵawo.
Wati wapulika kuti muwoli
wake yasomphola fumu, mnyamata
yula ngawakulanguruka kuti "Sono
ningatuma njani kwa fumu?"
Ngawakuyezga viyuni vyakupam-
banapambana. Ha-a!
Yazakaŵako njiŵa. Ngawaku-
yituma. Akuti,

*(Na mazgu ghakuzikitizga
kwakurongora kujigomezga:)*
"Ukapoke mphande zane za mu
vitende."
Njiŵa ngayikwiza kwa fumu.
Yili:
*(MWIMBI wakurongozga sumu
na mazgu ghakurongora nchen-
jezgo:)*
M: Chakum'potola kuku
Ŵ: Chakum'potola
M: Mphande yaŵene ya muvitende
Ŵ: Chakum'potola
Fumu yikuti,
(Na mazgu ghakutafula:)
"Akee, mphande nkhanthu uli?
Mwanakazi ngwakutowa chomeni
uyu." Yili na mphande za mu
vitende vule-vule.
Njiŵa ngayikukapereka.
Mnyamata yula ngawakuyitu-
maso, wali, "Kanipokere mphande
zane za mu makongono."
Njiŵa ngayikufikaso kwa fumu.
Yili:
M: Chakum'potola kuku
Ŵ: Chakum'potola
M: Mphande yaŵene ya m'makon-
gono
Ŵ: Chakum'potola
Fumu yikulorako chara kumuvu-
la mwanakazi yula mphande za
mumakongono.
Njiŵa ngayikutumikaso kukapo-
ka mphande za mu mawoko. Fumu
ngayikupereka kwambula kuka-
napo.
Pa umaliro mnyamata yula
ngawakutuma njiŵa kuti,
"Kanipokere mphande yane ya pa
mutu."

Njiŵa ngayikufikaso kwa fumu. Yili:

M: Chakum'potola kuku

Ŵ: Chakum'potola

M: Mphande yaŵene ya pa mutu

Ŵ: Chakum'potola

Fumu yili, "Ake-ake, pagonachi apa?" Yati waka topole mphande ya pa mutu, mbwenu khuni la chipombola zukuu!

(Pakuti zukuu, MWIMBI waku-tambazura mawoko kurongora ukuru wa khuni)

Mwanakazi wazgoka khuni!...

(Na mazgu ghakuhoya:)

Fumu yatondeka! Chamara.

7. Mwanakazi na Masumbi

ŴANTHU ŵakaya ku chisokole. Sono ghala ŵakuŵamba, mbwenu ngaŵakusanga masumbi ghanandi chomeni.

Sono pakuti ŵawone njala yaŵapweteka, mbwenu ngaŵakwamba kumwapo masumbi ghala. Ŵali,

(*MWIMBI wakuyowoya na mazgu ghakusekerera:*)
"A! Vinthu kunowa ivi!"
Ŵakamwa ŵakakhuta; kweni masumbi ghakakharaposo ghanandi chomeni.

Ŵanthu ŵala, pakughatemweska masumbi ghala chifukwa cha kunowa kwake, ŵakazomerezgana kuti nyengo zose para ŵiza kukuŵamba ŵazamumwangapo masumbi ghala m'paka ghamare.

(*Na mazgu ghakuchenjezga:*)
Kweni ŵakazomerezgana kuti ŵangaphaliranga munthu mnyake cha za masumbi ghala: Ŵakapanganaso kuti paŵavye yumoza wayeghere ku kaya nanga lingaŵa jisumbi limoza pera.

(*Na mazgu ghakurongora kususka:*)
A! Mnyawo yumoza wabisirizgako!

Ku kaya na mise akutola, akupa mwanakazi wake. Mwanakazi iryeirye. Ghala waryera mwanakazi yula akuti

(*Na mazgu ghakumeka:*)
"Afumu ŵane, vinthu vikunowa ivi mwe! Mukanirongore apo vili, nivimwenge madazi ghose."

Mwanarumi:
(*MWIMBI wakusunkhunya maphewa uku wakujuma, kurongora umo mwanarumi wakofyekera na icho wakakhumbanga muwoli wake:*)
"Mm! Mm! Mm! Ŵanyane ŵangukana. Ningakakurongora yayi."

Akuti,
(*Na mazgu ghakunyengerera:*)
"Yayi, pulizi kanirongorani."

Mwanarumi:
(*Na mazgu ghakujigowokera:*)
"Hee, ŵawoli ŵane ŵati nkhaŵarongore."

Pa ulendo.
(*Mwanakazi mkati mu ŵakutegherezga wali, "Nthengwa! Nthengwa njakuzirwa!")*
Ŵafika para. Ŵakwambako kumwa masumbi papara para. Mwanarumi wimilira patali nthe para (*MWIMBI wakurongora mtunda wakuyana na apo Mwanarumi wakimilira).*

(*Na mazgu ghakuchenjezga:*)
Cheneko chawuka nthena uko!
(*MWIMBI wakurongora nakamunwe mtunda utali*)
Mwanarumi wakuwona mfwiri wake pera. Akuphalira muwoli wake akuti:

(MWIMBI wakurongozga sumu na mazgu ghakusoka mwakudinginika:)

MWIMBI: Ewe we, he!

ŴAZOMEREZGI: Chidya-mtambo walilima, Chidyamtambo

M: Ewe we, he!

Ŵ: Chidyamtambo walilima, Chidyamtambo

M: Mwene wa masumbi ghake

Ŵ: Chidyamtambo walilima, Chidyamtambo

Ndipo akupokera mwanakazi akuti:

(MWIMBI wakurongozga sumu na mazgu ghakurongora kufwasa:)

M: Phwa! Kunowa!

Ŵ: Chidyamtambo walilima, Chidyamtambo

M: Phwa! Kunowa mwe!

Ŵ: Chidyamtambo walilima, Chidyamtambo.

Aaa, chikwiza nthena uko! Uum!

(Pakuti uum!, MWIMBI wakupanga mankhwinya pa maso uku watambazura mawoko, kurongora kofya na ukuru wa cheneko cha masumbi)

(Na mazgu ghakurongora kususka:)

Mbwenu aaa, mwanakazi wademwera papara.

Mwanarumi wakuchema:

M: Ewe we, he!

Ŵ: Chidyamtambo walilima, Chidyamtambo

M: Ewe we, he!

Ŵ: Chidyamtambo walilima, Chidyamtambo

M: Mwene wa masumbi ghake

Ŵ: Chidyamtambo walilima, Chi-

dyamtambo

Wali:

M: Phwa! Kunowa!

Ŵ: Chidyamtambo, walilima, Chidyamtambo

M: Phwa! Kunowa mwe!

Ŵ: Chidyamtambo walilima, Chidyamtambo

Mbwenu chikwiza nthena uko! Lililili! Mfwiri vwiku nkhanirankhanira. Aaa,

(MWIMBI wakukuŵa mapi kamoza, kurongora kuti vinthu vyasuzga:)

iyo yayi – watana papara para.

Mwanarumi wakuti "Ghala ŵakakana ŵanyane! Ndite uli ine?"

Chikwiza chikulilimira kula. Ati:

M: Ewe we, he!

Ŵ: Chidyamtambo walilima, Chidyamtambo

M: Ewe we, he!

Ŵ: Chidyamtambo walilima, Chidyamtambo

M: Mwene wa masumbi ghake

Ŵ: Chidyamtambo walilima, Chidyamtambo

Ati:

M: Phwa! Kunowa!

Ŵ: Chidyamtambo walilima, Chidyamtambo

M: Phwa! Kunowa mwe!

Ŵ: Chidyamtambo walilima, Chidyamtambo

(Na mazgu ghakuhoya:)

Mbwe chafika: Kokaa! Chili nayo kha! Mwanarumi pa thengere keŵe! – uyo, akuya ku kaya! Iwo kusu! Chamara.

THE SONGS

PREFACE TO THE SONGS

Upon first reading Tito Banda's manuscript of Malawian folktales, I was impressed with his efforts to capture the stylistic nuances of the master storyteller's performances. I resolved to do my best to rise to the same challenge: to do for the songs what Mr. Banda has done for the tales.

In refining Mjura Mkandawire's transcriptions, I have indicated as many musical nuances as possible, in the hope that these traditional folktales will continue to be retold and sung as richly as possible.

As I worked with the recording of Old Nyaviyuyi, I found that my understanding of, and relationship to, musical notation changed dramatically. In my mind, musical notation had always been a static medium from which unknown music could be extracted. Sometimes nuance of stylistic interpretation was evident, but more often the interpretation was left to the discretion and resources of the performer. Suddenly here were dynamic examples of rich oral expressions that had melody and rhythmic duration that had to be described visually so that others might one day retrieve them from the pages of this book to again transmit the cultural information that the original performer had in mind.

These traditional Malawian songs seriously challenged the descriptive ability of traditional western notation. There were many instances where the notation had not enough complexity or flexibility to really capture the fluidity of the performance. In those cases, only a visual approximation was possible. Where I created my own visual devices to better describe a nuance, a footnote has been included.

The rhythmic demands of the Chitumbuka language are very different from those of the English language, so although Mr Banda has attempted to fit the translations to the music, it is recommended that non-Chitumbuka speakers should make the effort to sing the songs in the original language. They are worth the effort. The pronunciation guide provided in the Introduction and at the beginning of each tale should be helpful.

Finally, I wish to give my thanks to Mr. Banda for allowing me the opportunity to learn about Old Nyaviyuyi's tales and songs. It has been my great joy to make some small contribution to the preservation of the folk music of Malawi in general, and these songs in particular.

The tales and songs encapsulate the essence of Malawian culture. It is through embracing our cultural heritage that we learn who we are as a people. Only then can we be strong enough to rise above our individual lives to contribute something of lasting value to others. Strong roots grow strong trees.

Andrea Matthews
Mzuzu, Malawi
July, 2006

NOTES ON THE SONGS

One of the most interesting outcomes of the hours spent listening to Old Nyaviyuyi was the gradual understanding that the meter of Malawian music functions differently from the western music which I am accustomed to hearing. Old Nyaviyuyi's singing is very fluid and flexible, with the text driving the rhythm and meter. Most of the songs seem to be in 9/8 or 12/8, yet seldom do they function as compound meters. The smallest beat units tend to be eighth notes (quavers), but the larger beats are often subdivided into duplets, rather than triplets. There is also a tendency to switch between the two. The fluid shifting between the duple and triple creates a very dynamic and compelling feeling in the songs.

In the following transcriptions, the beaming of the notes indicates the duple or triple nature of the melody. Mr. Mkandawire's convention of writing in the key of F has been retained. Once learned, all songs should be sung in the most comfortable range of the Narrator's voice.

Tale 1:   *A-ha-ha sefu yize pano*
      The upper neighbour in the melody on the word *sefu* in the first phrase is echoed in the melody later on the word *bwenkha,* though in the second instance, Old Nyaviyuyi does it in such a way that it seems to indicate the character's derision for *bwenkha* (vegetable relish.)

Tale 2:   *ŴaMdangu mwizaso*
      This is the piece that departed most radically from Mr. Mkandawire's transcription. It was the most rhythmically complex piece. After working on all the other songs, I had come to understand that the Chitumbuka language required meters that moved in eighth note (quaver) beats, and that phrases were often asymmetrical. The 4/4 meter of Mr. Mkandawire's version seemed too regular and symmetrical to fit Old Nyaviyuyi's performance. I started writing it afresh keeping in mind the stresses, but with no attempt to measure the melodic phrases. It took almost two weeks of daily listening and try-

76

ing various rhythms to describe the way Old Nyaviyuyi stretched syllables and rolled off the phrases for me to be able to finally arrive at the notation herein. In that single instant, the same meters became apparent in this song that had been seen in all the other songs, although in an alternating order.

Tale 3: *Wamchila wane dumuka*

The vitality of the first rhythm immediately captivates the listener. Then Old Nyaviyuyi expertly delays the text of the opening phrase from *wa mchila wane dumuka tila* to *mchila wane dumuka tila*. When the song is sung a second time, the *mchila wane dumuka tila* phrase is delayed and reduced still further to *dumuka tila* with its melody sung a step lower until it ends on the same note.

Tale 4: *Chati go!*

In notating this song, Mr. Mkandawire wrote it in 3/4, which adequately described the rhythm. I chose, however, to rewrite it in 12/8 to make apparent the underlying eighth note (quaver) pulse. The second time Old Nyaviyuyi sings this song, the call of *chati go!* rarely begins on a definite pitch, though the *go!* most often lands on the call's home tone.

Tale 4: *ŴaMakokota*

This song is sung as written the first time. In the second and third renditions, Old Nyaviyuyi substitutes the names of the other dogs for *ŵaMakokota: ŵaChimthiko* (ŵa-Chi-mthi-ko) and *Mwe ŵaNthoromi* (Mwe ŵa-Ntho-ro-mi), respectively.

Tale 4: *Kabayi Muyune*

The 7/8 measures in this song may be a function of the language: the "n" sound of *ndaruta* requiring a bit more time to execute, or it may be Old Nyaviyuyi's subtle way of emphasizing the phrase *ndaruta ndabaya* (translation: I went forth and slew it.)

Tale 5: *Hu-uuu! Ŵanthu ŵala*

The B-flats in the Narrator's part are very fluid and unstable. The notation is not very representative of how Old Nyaviyuyi bends them upward before sliding down off them. This deliberate instability of

77

tonality gives the phrase an emotional immediacy and greater depth of expression than would be possible had she settled on a single definite pitch.

Tale 6: *Ŵamama ŵane*

In one rendition of this song, when the unmarried brother calls his mother or wife, Old Nyaviyuyi sings the calls a minor third higher than the written melody to give the impression of a different, younger voice.

Tale 6: *Chakum'potola*

The fluidity of the alternation between the triple and duple feeling creates a rich tapestry of language in this song.

Tale 7: *Ewe we he!*

Grace notes are used to indicate the relative stress of the sounds that they indicate. When the duration of the grace note is the same as the note it is gracing, the pitches are of the same length, though stressed differently. When they are of different durations, their proportional relationship should be observed while keeping the relative stress in mind.

A-ha-ha sefu yize pano
(Ah-ha-ha let an eland come now)

ŴaMdangu mwizaso
(O Mdangu, you've come back)

Wamchila wane dumuka
(O my tail get cut)

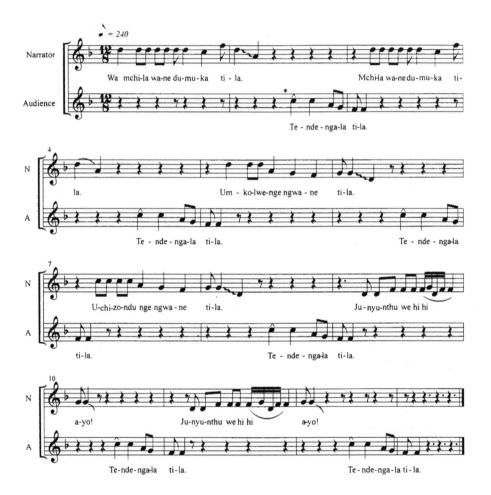

* Wherever this symbol (^) appears above a note, it indicates that the pitch is bent upward slightly.

Chati go!
(It goes *go!*)

ŴaMakokota

(O Makokota)

Kabayi Muyune

(Go and slay Fierce Bird)

Ka - ba - yi Ji - wu - nde - mbo.

Hee nya - ma - li - mba te ma.

Nda - ru - ta nda - ba - ya.

Hee nya - ma - li - mba te - ma.

Hu-uuu! Ŵanthu ŵala

(Hu-uuu! There's a village)

Ŵamama ŵane

(Mother of mine)

Ŵamama = Mother

Ŵawoli = Wife

Chakum'potola

* In the recorded version, Old Nyaviyuyi sang all the different *mphande* beads into one rendition of the song. In another version heard by the author, Old Nyaviyuyi sang the entire song four times during the tale, each time with a different *mphande* phrase sung as notated above.

The first time: *mphande yawene ya mu vitende* (ankle *mphande.*)
The second time: *mphande yawene ya mu mawoko* (wrist *mphande.*)
The third time: *mphande yawene ya ku malundi* (knee *mphande.*)
The fourth time: *mphande yawene ya ku mutu* (head *mphande.*)

Ewe we he!

(Look, my poor dear!)

Printed in the United States
By Bookmasters